MILNER CRAFT SERIES

VICTORIAN EMBROIDERY

MILNER CRAFT SERIES

VICTORIAN EMBROIDERY

ROBBYN MACDONALD

SALLY MILNER PUBLISHING

Dedication
TO LACHLAN AND TAYLOR

First published in 1993 by
Sally Milner Publishing Pty Ltd
558 Darling Street
Rozelle NSW 2039 Australia

Reprinted 1994 (twice)

© Robbyn Macdonald, 1993

Design by Wing Ping Tong
Illustrations by Bryony Dade
Photography by Neil Lorimer
Styling by Judy Ostergaard
Typeset in Australia by Asset Typesetting Pty Ltd
Printed in Australia by Impact Printing, Melbourne

National Library of Australia
Cataloguing-in-Publication data:

Macdonald, Robbyn
    Victorian embroidery

    ISBN 1 86351 110 5

    1. Embroidery – Patterns. 2. Needlework, Victorian. 3.
Decoration and ornament – Victorian style. I. Title. (Series:
Milner craft series).

746.44041

CONTENTS

ABOUT THE AUTHOR

My first experience of embroidery was watching my Grandmother who spent painstaking hours embroidering the finest detail on superb fabrics she had collected.

I dabbled with it until I started school where I was keenly interested in all aspects of craft, especially embroidery and painting.

I continued painting over the years (and still do) and then, three and a half years ago, attended embroidery classes and became 'addicted'. I was commissioned to design and embroider several pieces for a book, *Elegant Embroidery.* These can be seen on pages 48 (Christmas tablecloth and napkins), and pages 62 to 67 (nightgown, robe, slippers and lingerie bag) of the book.

I began teaching embroidery to several friends one night each week and then, after an article in the magazine *House and Garden*, and through recommendations passed by word of mouth, my classes rapidly increased to six classes per week and daytime workshops for country, interstate and local women. My classes and commissions keep me extremely busy and fulfilled.

I have an incredibly supportive husband, who has his own thriving company and who doubles as chef and house husband very successfully and cheerfully!

ACKNOWLEDGEMENTS

This embroidery book has been an integral part of my life for the past couple of years, and what seemed like a mammoth task in writing it, has given me immense pleasure and satisfaction and has truly been a labour of love. It would not be complete, however, without the following acknowledgements:

My sincere thanks to my best friend, Alison Brewer, for her endless support and assistance, and for being the wonderful friend she is.

Sincere thanks also to Janet Rowe.

My thanks to Dorothy Jurgens — cushion maker extraordinaire at 80 years of age — for making up all my cushions.

My thanks to Eric Baker, Angela Warren and Lin Qin Zhiang from Port Melbourne Prints and Framing, for their assistance and attention to detail — at a moment's notice.

To my students and friends for their continuing enthusiasm, kindness and constant inspiration.

My thanks to Bryony Dade for her elaborate and beautifully detailed sketches — her kind and gentle nature shows through in her work.

My thanks to Thelma Wenke, a dear friend, for her untiring help and kindness, and for having the tenacity to be my longest-serving student!

To my dear Aunt Valerie and Uncle Oscar Ferguson and family. Val for her invaluable advice and good taste, caring support and constant assistance, and Oscar for his good humour and unfailing support in caring for us all.

I would like to also pass on my sincere thanks to the following people:

Joe Murray for his continued support and valuable advice from the start of the project; Frances Hylton for her patience in deciphering illegible scrawl; Andrea Rumpf for her gift of beautiful antique lace; Lance Roach and Andrew Mitchell, Gills Grendon Nursery; Robyn Buccheri for a location shot in her garden; Mary Lansley, Wai Marie Florist, Dingley; Jenni Thompson for the kind loan of her old English pram; Val Philpott for embroidering the tooth fairy pillow; Elaine Lee, Le Collections.

My special thanks to Neil Lorimer and Judy Ostergaard for their expertise and professionalism.

To Sally Milner and staff for their enthusiasm and for giving me the opportunity to write this book.

And finally, my love and deep gratitude to my husband Stuart. Without his patience and tremendous support this book would not have been possible.

ALL YOU NEED

I was inspired to write this embroidery book for several reasons. One of them was that after teaching hundreds of women I have discovered the most difficult aspect of the craft is actually thinking of the design. My book shows each design clearly and comprehensively and the stitch glossary is in great detail. This means someone who is totally new to embroidery can pick up my book and learn. Advanced embroiderers can use this book as an inspiration, as well as a means to increase their skills.

I also feel an important aspect of this book is the comprehensive list of materials. (More often than not books fail to reveal their source of materials and this can be frustrating.)

The materials used are extremely varied. To mention a few: wool, DMC cotton, silk threads of many textures from matt to shiny, rayon ribbon, silk and satin ribbon and taffeta ribbon with metal edges. I also use a large variety of antique silks, ribbons, laces and braids and feel it an integral part of this book to list stockists of these materials, which are exclusive to my book.

There is a resurgence of interest in craft and embroidery and my wish is that this book, with its beautiful and unusual designs, combined with easy to understand, step-by-step instructions and the extensive list of products and suppliers, will fill a space.

My desire, is that *Victorian Embroidery* will be a book to cherish.

FABRICS AND MATERIALS

There is a beautiful assortment of fabrics to choose from today. Keep in mind when selecting a particular fabric, whether you will be wanting the finished product specifically as a decorative piece, or to use. For example, if you want to liven up a corner of the living room with cushions to sit on, choose a sturdy fabric that can be laundered easily, like an upholstery damask or something similar. Don't be afraid to use an upholstery moiré fabric as it is a robust material and wears well. Your choice of design for such an area should be restricted to a flatter look and in such instances you would not place ribbon roses that could be flattened by being leaned on constantly.

On the other hand, for that special corner of the bedroom or sitting room, or to adorn a favourite antique, the sky's the limit and you can choose from any of the delicate silks and taffetas available.

The materials I have used in my designs are mainly Thai silk and upholstery damask.

Thai silk is a beautiful fabric to work with and comes in a rainbow of colours.

A very handy aspect of using Thai silk is that you can match the colours with your selection of braids. No matter what colour braid you choose I guarantee you will match it perfectly with a Thai silk shade. Another interesting feature with Thai silk is often a colour will be shot with another colour, so you may have gold silk that, when moved, will change to green — this gives a stunning look to embroidered cushions, especially if ruched in the contrasting silk of green shot with gold.

The *upholstery damask* I have used on a variety of cushions and framed pieces gives an excellent result, especially if using ribbons, braids and decorative objects. The texture and weight of the fabric lends itself to the use of these heavier objects and you can really go to town — as shown in the cover design. The fabric is sturdy enough to hold the heaviness of all the ribbon work.

I also use *upholstery moiré taffeta*. It is important to use upholstery moiré as you will notice that

when compared to dress moiré it has much more vitality. This is also suitable for heavier work, but accepts happily your most delicate stitches.

Silk dupion is an interesting fabric to use. I use it on the odd occasion I want a more textured background. It can give your work a more rustic effect.

Other materials I am very fond of, but which are not shown in this book, are the *silk tartans and checks*. The most striking results can be achieved by matching ribbons and yarns to tartans and checks and embroidering circlets of flowers and ribbon roses directly on to the tartan and ruching in a contrasting material. These are wonderful designs for winter warmth, and complement any fireplace.

Silk organza is also a beautifully delicate fabric to work with and is usually shown adorned with shadow embroidery. The single piece in this book combines a little shadow embroidery with ribbon and finer embroidery. Although silk organza is a light sheer fabric and very flimsy, it holds heavier embroidery work well and gives your work a very soft and dreamy effect.

When using organza, the crucial factor in achieving a professional and attractive finish is to be meticulous in neatening the back of your work. Care must be taken to tidy up loose threads and hide ribbon ends as the front of your work will give you away. It is a tedious task but well worth the effort.

BRAIDS, TASSELS, LACES AND BAUBLES

There are myriad braids and laces to be found in specialty and 'old world' shops. I have used a variety of these, including small trinkets found on my travels. I tend to buy interesting braids and baubles when I see them because I always find just the perfect place to put them. If you build up a nice collection of these, you will always be ready to begin a new piece of embroidery and have everything at hand.

Since starting embroidery I have become an avid collector of all sorts of interesting pieces. I mainly collect antique laces, braids and baubles but I have a wonderful collection of new ribbons and braids as well. It is really left up to your imagination as to what you can use on your creative designs. As shown in this book, anything goes, from old crystal buttons to filigree pieces, pearls, jet buttons, and antique fringing, small bread dough pieces, old silk flowers and the like.

Good luck hunting!

THREADS AND RIBBONS

There are so many textures of threads and ribbons used in my designs and for that reason I have included a ribbon glossary. Half the battle in achieving a design in a book is being able to locate the exact materials.

The main yarns used are DMC cottons, made in France, and Birch and Macdougall's silk ribbon made in Japan.

The variety of ribbons I use, range from the double-sided satin example to Macdougall's and the Japanese Mokuba brand which has a most stunning assortment of ribbons.

I also use a large number of antique ribbons and yarns — not readily available but easy to locate if you are interested in searching through suitable shops.

I use a variety of yarns I have obtained from overseas travels and some of these are available by mail order from me. I substitute these with readily available materials for easy access.

NEEDLES

For most of the embroidery throughout this book I have used Birch crewel needles size 3/9. I find these needles fill most of my needs and their range in eyelet size means I can change the needle to suit thread and silk ribbon size. Another advantage in using these needles is that the needle point is

not as sharp as other needles. (I find every now and then, when using a student's needle, I can always tell if it is not a crewel — I tend to prick myself as I am using it — I am very accustomed to the crewel.)

I use the Birch Chenille needles size 18/24 for threading ribbons through. The size of the eyelet is perfect for wide ribbon use.

BIRCH FRAY STOPPER

This is another product used to make life a bit easier.

This small tube of glue is a must when it comes to using Thai silk — to embroider on Thai silk without it is a nightmare. It is very easy to use as you just squeeze it around the edge of material and wait 10 to 15 minutes for it to dry — the silk will not fray and your cushion maker will thank you!

Another handy hint when using delicate and flimsy fabrics like Thai silk, is to iron on a lightweight *woven* interfacing. This gives the fabric support and makes it much easier to handle. The brand I find most useful is the Birch American brand.

When using wide ribbons, as I do in many of my designs, it can be difficult to pull the needle and ribbon through the material. To make this easier, use a stiletto to punch a hole in the fabric and then your needle with ribbon will glide through. Stilettos are available from most craft and haberdashery stores.

Taking Care of your Work

CLEANING

I am asked how to care for and clean embroidered cushions many times. If and when the need arises, specialist dry cleaners do a superb job of caring for and cleaning these pieces.

It is a good idea to discuss the cleaning with your dry cleaner beforehand, making sure to mention *not* to press the item. This may sound like commonsense, but you would be surprised how often I have seen beautiful embroidered ribbon roses pressed flat as a tack! If you find a good dry cleaner you can be assured of a beautiful result.

As far as the baby items are concerned, I always use materials that are easy to hand wash. Damask, lawn and checked cotton fabrics are lovely to use and easily laundered.

The baby blanket is kept beautiful by washing in Martha Gardners Wool Mix and drying flat. Even if you decide to use silk threads on your baby blanket, using this product will assure you of a good result.

FRAMING

When you have completed your design it is very important that the fruit of your labour is shown to its best advantage. This is where framing comes in and there are a few guidelines to guarantee a successful result. I cannot stress enough the importance of having your work framed by a specialist. I have seen work virtually ruined by poor framing and improper stretching. After all the hours you have spent creating your finished piece,

it deserves the attention of a specialist framer —
after all it is now an heirloom, and often a specialist
is significantly less expensive than a novice
competitor.

The most important area of framing is to ensure
the work is stretched properly. This gives your
embroidery a smooth, even background. If care is
not taken in this area, the work can look uneven,
lopsided and have a rippling effect.

There are so many options available in mounting
and framing needlework and the frame (moulding)
you choose should enhance a beautiful embroidery.
I have selected a wide variety of mouldings to
demonstrate the different effects achieved in each
embroidery. In some cases two or more mouldings
can be combined to add a brilliant new dimension
to the design and I have done this on one of my
pieces.

Once you have chosen the frame the next step
is to decide on whether you wish to use a
mattboard. There are hundreds of colours and
many different textures available, including gold,
silver and even sueded board. Mattboard not only
provides a decorative quality, but also has a
practical function in protecting your artwork.

The colour and type of mattboard you choose
depends on the colour and design of your work
and this is where a professional framer who gives
attention to such detail is invaluable.

Another creative and specialised service that
can be obtained is the shadow, or 'object box',
to hold a three-dimensional item. I have used this
style of framing on several of my designs and the
result is beautiful. An object box can be built quite
simply, or it can be designed with rich fabrics and
woods for a more elaborate treatment. With my
designs, my framer has paid great care and attention
to detail by painting the inside moulding in the
exact shade of the fabric used. When it comes to
object boxes many exciting things are possible.

Another idea is to hunt for interesting antique
frames to house your embroidery. Antique and
older frames make an unusual feature of your work
and look fabulous.

NSPIRATIONAL VICTORIAN LACE

This section, consisting of cushions and one framed piece, demonstrates beautifully the effective use of antique laces and braids, tassels and ribbons, buttons and baubles. You can find materials like these if you hunt in antique shops, bric-a-brac and opportunity shops and bazaars and markets. You can still achieve a beautiful cushion by using new products readily available. Some of these are in the stockists' section at the back of this book.

With a little imagination you can create a superb heirloom using materials from a bygone era. Half the enjoyment is procuring these delicate materials, each with a story of its own, and with each piece discovered you will find the perfect home for it to adorn.

The shapes and sizes of the many laces found will immediately determine their position on your future creation. For instance, a Victorian collar becomes a halo for soft ribbon work. A lovely piece of Victorian lace becomes the central feature of a soft pink cushion surrounded by roses. If the shape of your lace is quite lengthy it then lends itself to surround the edge of a cushion and you can then adorn it how you see fit. A small sample of Victorian beading and tassels fits snugly around a petite hat pin cushion.

So, always carefully examine the shape and length of lace and you will determine its place on your next creation.

VICTORIAN LACE CUSHION

This cushion is a beautiful way to display a lovely piece of Victorian lace, but the same effect can be achieved by using a favourite modern piece.

MATERIALS

1.5 m (1⅔ yd) palest pink Thai silk

26 cm x 23 cm (10″ x 9″) panel of lace
(easy to find in old wares' shops)

3 m (3⅓ yd) of soft pink ribbon, 25 mm (1″)
wide (I have used old seam binding)

1 m (1¼ yd) of softest pink double-sided satin
ribbon, 8 mm (¼″) wide

DMC Perle green thread col. 3

4 m (4⅓ yd) silk ribbon col. 162 pink 4 mm
(⅛″) wide

2 m (2½ yd) silk ribbon col. 73 green, 4 mm
(⅛″) wide

METHOD

Cut 34 cm x 37 cm (13″ x 14½″) fabric and use fray stopper around edge to prevent fraying.

Stitch lace panel in centre of fabric. Using softest pink double-sided satin ribbon, cover each end of lace panel and stitch in place by hand. Make 2 pink bows from seam binding and stitch at top and bottom of panel. Using Perle DMC no. 3 col. and working in stem stitch, form a vine effect over double-sided satin ribbon on each side of cushion. Using pure silk ribbon 7 mm (¼″) and seam binding, make 4 ribbon roses for each side in both colours and stitch as shown, alternating the colours.

Make 4 ribbon roses in double-sided satin ribbon and sew 2 each side in middle edge of lace, placing pure silk rose in between. Work 3 silk buds each side of panel. Using green thread, work lazy daisy leaves around vine and roses.

Taking green silk ribbon, work straight stitch leaves on roses where shown on diagram.

Make up with 11 cm (4¼″) frill.

VICTORIAN MUSK PINK CUSHION

WITH BLACK LACE AND TASSELS

The materials used in this cushion are mostly Victorian. The beautiful black lace panel is circa 1890 and in superb condition. The pink crystal buttons with pearl centre and jets are circa 1930. The tiny pink beads making up bows are circa 1920.

MATERIALS

1.5 m (1⅔ yd) musk pink Thai silk
160 cm (1⅔ yd) panel of rich black lace, 12 cm (4½″) wide
2 m (2½ yd) black velvet ribbon, 3.5 cm (1¼″) wide
4 jet buttons
4 pink crystal buttons
Pink beads
1 beading needle
Tassels

You can find materials like these if you hunt in antique shops, bric-a-brac, opportunity shops and bazaars and markets. You can still achieve a beautiful cushion by using new products readily available. Some of these are in the stockists' section at the back of this book.

METHOD

Use fray stopper to prevent material fraying.

Cut 38 cm x 38 cm (15″ x 15″) square of musk pink fabric. Take the lace panel and lay it around the edge of your material, leaving 2 cm (¾″) of fabric for seam allowance. As you lay the lace around the square of each corner you will have a loose flap of lace. I did not cut the lace at these corners but made an inverted pleat by folding the middle of the lace at each corner into a triangle shape and hand stitching in place. If you are using old lace it would be a shame to cut into a beautiful heirloom.

Pin the lace around the edge of fabric — this is quite a fiddly job but well worth the effort. Stitch securely with black cotton, making sure all corners are sewn securely. Once in place, make 4 bows from black velvet ribbon and stitch to top edge of triangle pleat.

Using beading needle or very fine needle, thread pink beads to form triangles as shown, making 2 loops of beads at each end that resemble bows when stitched in place.

Sew jet buttons in each corner of square as shown and pink crystal buttons on bows. Sew tassels in place, and the result is quite dramatic.

VICTORIAN MUSK PINK HAT PIN CUSHION

I was fortunate to find a superb piece of Victorian beading fringe with jet beads and two black tassels all intact. It was very dusty so I gently soaked it in Martha Gardners Wool Mix and cleaned it with a soft toothbrush. The result was a wonderful surprise of shiny black beads and tassels ready to adorn a small cushion.

The central motif of this cushion is a Victorian circlet. This was made using grosgrain ribbon and pleating it to form a circle. I added a touch of glitter by sewing an old circle of sequins and a bead to the centre.

If you cannot find a suitable old piece of fringing you can buy beading from department and specialty stores and add jet buttons to it. With a little imagination you can create an original piece of work that is beautiful.

METHOD

Stitch fringing around edge of cushion leaving 2 cm (¾″) for seam. Sew black velvet bow at join and black tassels at either end.

Sew central motif in place.

My Auntie, on seeing the finished product, suggested it be used for a collection of old hat pins — what better place for them!

GOLD CUSHION WITH 1950S' BRAID

MATERIALS

0.5 m (20″) green-gold Thai silk or silk to complement the colour of your braid

20.5 cm x 18 cm (8″ x 7″) green Thai silk (or equivalent for centre square)

1½ m (1¾ yd) of braid

2 m (2½ yd) gold satin ribbon, 15 mm (¾″) wide

1 m (1¼ yd) single-sided Mokuba velvet ribbon, 25 mm (1″) wide

2 m (2½ yd) green/gold rayon Mokuba ribbon, 25 mm (1″) wide

1.5 m (1⅔ yd) Mokuba gold metallic ribbon

4 metal filigree corner pieces

Birch gold Glista thread

DMC 834 for wattle

Tassels/braid

METHOD

Cut 37 cm x 35 cm (14½″ x 14″) square and use fray stopper on edges.

Sew 20.5 cm x 18 cm (8″ x 7″) green silk or equivalent colour in centre of cushion.

Sew braid around edge of centre fabric.

Take lengths of braid 23 cm (9″) long and place one end on top of other. Secure on adjacent corners as shown. Make 2 rayon bows and sew on top of these. Make 2 bows with Mokuba single-sided velvet ribbon and stitch in place on opposite corners.

Make 4 large tea roses, as shown in Techniques (pages 77–84) and sew on top of bows.

Using velvet ribbon, make 2 looped leaves and stitch in place on single rose corners. On opposite corners make 4 small roses with metallic gold ribbon and sew in place.

Using complementary colours and Glista thread, embroider flowers as shown at 2 corners of work.

Sew metal corners in place.

Make up cushion with piping and complementary tassels or braid.

CREAM CUSHION WITH OLD RIBBON HEART

MATERIALS

1.5 m (1⅔ yd) cream damask

1.5 m (1⅔ yd) old soft green ribbon, 3 cm (1⅛″) wide, for heart

0.5 m (20″) apricot ribbon, 12 mm (½″) wide (not satin)

1 m (1¼ yd) cream double-sided satin ribbon, 8 mm (¼″) wide

3 m (3⅓ yd) pure silk ribbon col. 157 4 mm (⅛″) wide

3 m (3⅓ yd) pure silk ribbon col. 162 4 mm (⅛″) wide

1 m (1¼ yd) Mokuba sheer satin-edged cream ribbon, 15 mm (¾″) wide

1 m (1¼ yd) Mokuba sheer metallic apricot ribbon with cream metallic edge, 15 mm (¾″) wide

DMC Colours: Ecru, 754 Apricot, 525 Green

DMC Perle no. 5 col.

Small heart motif with centre cut out — dipped in tea to give muted colour

METHOD

Cut 32 cm x 32 cm (12½″ x 12½″) for cushion leaving 2 cm (¾″) for seam allowance. Draw heart template on fabric and stitch soft green ribbon around heart at inner edge of ribbon, leaving enough ribbon at bottom to tie a bow.

Make a large tea rose in cream Mokuba ribbon and metallic ribbon as contrasting petals and secure in centre of bow.

Sew heart motif in centre of ribbon heart and embroider bullion buds in DMC 754 (2 strands 10

wraps) around inside of lace. With 1 strand DMC 524 embroider lazy daisy leaves at base of each of bud.

Make 17 ribbon roses in alternate colours and sew around soft green ribbon as shown. Using pure silk ribbon, work ribbon buds around inside of heart alternating the colour and embroidering bullions as shown. With DMC 524 using 1 strand, embroider fly stitch around bullion buds.

With stranded cotton embroider lazy daisy leaves on all silk buds.

Make cushion up with 12 cm (4½‴) frill and contrasting piping.

Left to right: Victorian lace cushion; Cream cushion with old ribbon heart; caramel Victorian lace cushion

Victorian musk pink cushion with black lace tassels

Victorian musk pink hat pin cushion

Sensuous ocelot cushion

Framed Victorian collar

Top left to right: **Soft pastel vase and cream bask**
Middle left to right: **Gold Arabian vase; Wisteria v**
Bottom: **Gold basket of floppy gallica roses**

CARAMEL VICTORIAN LACE CUSHION

MATERIALS

68 cm (26½″) length of lace, 14 cm (5½″) wide
2 m (2½ yd) caramel Thai silk
4 m (4⅓ yd) caramel single-sided satin ribbon,
    1 cm (½″) wide
DMC Perle 950
DMC Perle 407
DMC Perle 732
DMC 3011 for fly stitch on buds, 1 strand

METHOD

Cut 52 cm x 39 cm (20½″ x 15″) of caramel fabric, using fray stopper around edges. Cut lace panel in half taking care not to damage pattern. This can be achieved quite easily if you very carefully snip in between the lace pattern, cutting away the loose ends and dabbing in places with fray stopper when you feel it may fray.

Sew both lace pieces about 16 cm (6½″) apart onto fabric.

Take 2 lengths of caramel ribbon 44 cm (17″) long and tie 4 knots across each length evenly apart (about 8 cm [3″]).

Stitch ribbon to top edge of lace along, both sides securely. Make 6 ribbon roses and sew in place over 2 knots and in centre on each ribbon length. Using Perle colours, embroider straight stitch buds out from each rose and attaching with 1 strand of DMC 3011 to roses, with lazy daisy leaves each side.

Using green Perle embroider large lazy daisy leaves around roses.

Make cushion up with very simple tight ruche, making the beautiful lace the total feature.

Victorian Collar

This piece was made by separating a Victorian collar to frame and feature the delicate embroidery and initial inside.

MATERIALS

45 cm x 50 cm (18″ x 20″) dusky pink fabric
  (I used damask)
Victorian or new collar
4 m (4⅓ yd) of pure silk ribbon col. 162 7 mm
  (⅛″) wide
Bullion buds DMC 778 2 strands
Pale green lazy daisy leaves DMC 524 1 strand
Moss green lazy daisy leaves DMC 3022 1
  strand
Madeira silk thread 0815 straight stitch buds 2
  strands
Pure silk ribbon col. 73 3 mm (⅛″) wide

METHOD

If using an old collar you will notice that it may be joined down the centre and is stiffened with celluloid. Snip carefully to separate collar and cut away celluloid. Stitch 2 pieces onto fabric to form a soft halo for your embroidery to be displayed.

Using pure silk 162, thread up on wide-eyed needle, stitch in a running stitch around base of lace. Bring needle up at top of lace and back through fabric next to where ribbon has just been brought through to form first loop of bow — repeat 1 cm (½″) across to form 2nd loop and work 2 straight stitches in centre to complete bow.

Bring ribbon out at edge of bow and leave 15 cm (6″) to stitch in place. To achieve the rippled effect, as you stitch in place starting at the top

near bow gently push ribbon after each stitch and hold in place while doing next stitch. Do this method 3 more times as shown.

Using pure silk 162, make up 6 small ribbon roses and secure in place using green pure silk 73 for ribbon leaves. Embroider Madeira silk buds with DMC 524 fly stitches to secure.

Using DMC 778, work 17 bullion buds in between silk running stitch and stem stitch vine around work using DMC 3022. Around each bud embroider lazy daisy leaves and straight stem in 1 strand DMC 3022.

Embroider initial in centre of work in DMC Ecru.

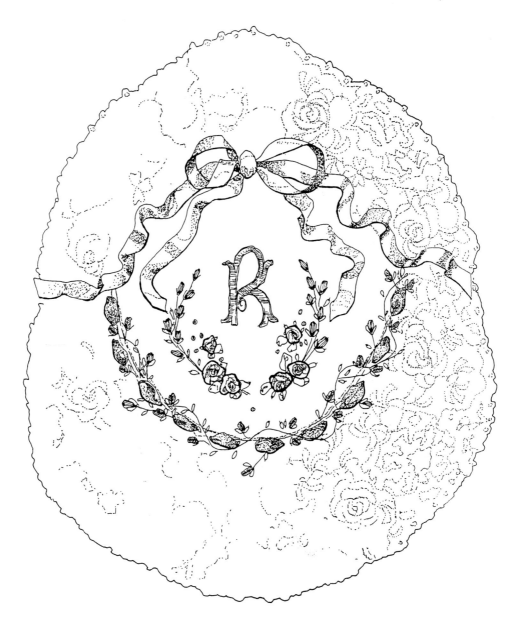

BASKETS, VASES AND URNS

WISTERIA VASE

For some stitches I have used Chinese silk thread available by mail order. DMC colours have been substituted if this is a problem.

All pure silk is 4 mm (⅛″) wide unless otherwise stated.

MATERIALS

46 cm x 46 cm (18″ x 18″) rich cream damask
1.5 m (1⅔ yd) gold rope braid
Setacolour gold fabric paint
Glista Birch gold thread
Ribbon as shown in ribbon glossary
5 m (5⅓ yd) each of pure silk ribbon colours, all 4 mm (⅛″) wide
DMC Colours Wisteria: 550 Deep Purple, 552 Purple, 208 Deep mauve, 209 Mauve, 210 Lilac, 211 Light lilac, 3041 Mixed purple, 3042, 367 Green
1st Lavender: 3 strands each of 340, 210, stems 2 strands 3053
2nd Lavender: 3 strands each of 3022, 3041 stems 2 strands 3022
3rd Lavender: 6 strands 209 only, DMC 3022 stems 2 strands
Wattle: Pure silk ribbon col. 15, made up of French knots, DMC 934 leaves and stems
Blue Bells: Pure silk col. 117, DMC 367 green for stem, stamens 1 strand 934, 1 strand 907 (or Chinese silk thread available from Robbyn Macdonald)

Daisies: Pure silk ribbon col. 13 — petals, Pure silk ribbon green col. 20 — leaves and stems, DMC 782 straight stitch for centre, DMC white French knots
Rose Buds: Pure silk ribbon centre col 163, Pure silk ribbon petals col. 162
Lilies: 2.5 m (2⅔ yd) double-sided satin ribbon cream 22 mm (1″) wide, DMC 782 for stamen, green rayon ribbon for petals, DMC 367 for stems
Lilacs: Deep purple rayon ribbon, Chinese silk thread or substitute — DMC 550 outer bullions, DMC 934 1 strand for stems
Yellow Buds: Chinese silk thread or substitute DMC 907, DMC 934 for stems and leaves

METHOD

Draw urn template onto fabric and stitch gold rope braid around edge, curling it into a circle at each end. Using gold Glista thread, embroider feet in long straight stitches. Paint inside urn with gold Setacolour and allow to dry (usually several hours) or you can place work face down on an old cloth and iron the back to dry paint instantly! (I am always too impatient to wait for the paint to dry so I use this method.)

The next step is to fill the vase with the largest flowers first and these are the tea and ribbon roses. Make them in the colours as shown and stitch them in place, attaching ribbon leaves in between where shown.

The next stage is to make the lilies and sew in place, embroidering stems in stem stitch up to roses.

Embroider wisteria, lilacs, daisies and lavender in that order as shown, then finish with remaining flowers to fill in remaining spaces.

Ribbon Glossary

50 cm (20″) emerald green taffeta ribbon 5 mm (¼″) wide

50 cm (20″) purple taffeta ribbon 50 mm (2″) wide

50 cm (20″) lime green taffeta ribbon 50 mm (2″) wide

1 m (1¼ yd) plum wire-edged ribbon 25 mm (1″) wide

1 m (1¼ yd) green wire-edged ribbon 25 mm (1″) wide

5 m (5⅓ yd) green rayon ribbon 7 mm (¼″) wide

3 m (3⅓ yd) purple rayon ribbon 7 mm (¼″) wide

1 m (1¼ yd) deep yellow wire-edged ribbon 38 mm (1½″) wide

1 m (1¼ yd) gold double-sided satin ribbon 13 mm (¾″) wide

50 cm (20″) variegated purple/green taffeta wire-edged ribbon 48 mm (1⅞″) wide

50 cm (20″) plum rayon ribbon 22 mm (⅞″) wide

1 m (1¼ yd) plum nylon ribbon with dark plum edge 10 mm (½″) wide

1 m (1¼ yd) yellow nylon ribbon with dark plum edge 10 mm (½″) wide

2 m (2½ yd) purple nylon ribbon with yellow edge 10 mm (½″) wide

1 m (1¼ yd) green one-sided velvet Mokuba ribbon 25 mm (1″) wide

50 cm (20″) mauve nylon ribbon 25 mm (1″) wide

GOLD ARABIAN VASE

MATERIALS

35 cm x 35 cm (14″ x 14″) purple silk
Ribbons as listed in glossary
DMC 934 1 strand for stems
DMC 733 2 strands for stems
Glista Birch gold thread
Chinese silk thread available by mail order from Robbyn Macdonald, or substitute:
DMC 550 Deep purple 6 strands, DMC 834 6 strands
Setacolour gold paint
Setacolour purple paint (if required)
6 gold round beads

2 m (2½ yd) burgundy wire-edged ribbon 25 mm (1″) wide
1 m (1¼ yd) plum rayon ribbon 22 mm (⅞″) wide
3 m (3⅓ yd) Mokuba single-sided satin ribbon gold 15 mm (¾″) wide
3 m (3⅓ yd) purple rayon ribbon 15 mm (¾″) wide
4 m (4⅓ yd) dark green rayon ribbon 15 mm (¾″) wide
2 m (2½ yd) Mokuba rayon lime ribbon 15 mm (¾″) wide
4 m (4⅓ yd) pure silk ribbon col. no. 72, 4 mm (⅛″) wide
variegated chenille thread (purple)
1 m (1¼ yd) gold satin cord
50 cm (20″) interesting gold braid

METHOD

Draw template of Arabian vase onto fabric and paint vase and handles gold. You can shade vase slightly with Setacolour purple paint, but this is not necessary. Allow to dry overnight (or iron back as for Wisteria Vase).

Using gold satin cord, sew around gold handles and feet using tacking stitch. With Glista thread, outline cord in stem stitch and sew small gold beads in each circle of cording.

With gold trimming sew along base of vase as shown and outline with purple variegated velvet thread. Fill vase with vibrant tea roses and buds, as shown in stitch glossary.

RIBBON GLOSSARY

1 m (1¼ yd) plum-coloured, wire-edged ribbon 40 mm (1½″) wide

VICTORIAN VASE

I have tried to create a Victorian Old World Vase (as shown on the cover) with the help of some beautiful old and antique laces, braids and buttons.

The unique buttons are made with shiny sequins which give them an interesting sparkle. I have also used an old-world bread dough brooch, the outer case of which has been cast from an antique piece.

I have used a very fine antique gold tulle for the vase body.

Although I have used mostly old materials in this vase, you can easily replace them with new ones.

MATERIALS

60 cm x 75 cm (24" x 30") piece rich upholstery damask

70 cm (28") gold braid for vase outer edge

50 cm (20") antique burnt gold braid or equivalent new braid for inner edge of vase

small piece of antique lace or equivalent for table cloth

50 cm (20") gold cord to separate outer and inner braid

5 apricot heart-shape crystal beads

small piece of gold tulle — I have used an antique piece of gold tulle. (You can substitute with a fine white tulle painted with gold fabric paint)

2 m (2½ yd) of gold bullion thread or fine gold braid or thread used in cross-cross pattern over vase

7 apricot pearl beads

1 bread dough old-world brooch or equivalent interesting piece

2 interesting buttons
2 tassels
2 filigree corner pieces

FLOWERS

2 m (2½ yd) matt dusky pink ribbon 2.5 cm (1″) wide

2 m (2½ yd) dusky pink Mokuba satin-edged ribbon 1.5 cm (¾″) wide

75 cm (30″) beige single-sided satin ribbon 4 cm (1½″) wide

3 m (3⅓ yd) green Mokuba organza ribbon with gold stripe 1.5 cm (¾″) wide

1.5 m (1⅔ yd) green rayon ribbon 1 cm (½″) wide

3 m (3⅓ yd) 7 mm (¼″) pure silk ribbon col. 162

Gold buds — 1 m (1¼ yd) gold rayon ribbon 1 cm (½″) wide

DMC 834 6 strands for straight stitches either side of gold rayon buds and bullion buds at end of drop

Pink ribbon buds — 3 m (3⅓ yd) pure silk ribbon 7 mm (¼″) wide col. 162

DMC 225 6 strands for bullion and either side of pink buds, and 1 strand for finer bullion stitches at end of drop

Madeira white stranded cotton for bullions at end of drop

DMC 3012 1 strand for stems and lazy daisy leaves

Lilacs — I have used old threads for these but you can substitute DMC 3042 3 strands and DMC 3041 6 strands and work French knots starting with darker colour and finishing with smaller knots at tips

Mauve straight stitch buds — I have used an old linen thread substitute DMC 3041 6 strands pure silk 4 mm (⅛″) ribbon col. 56 for straight stitch leaves either side. DMC 733 1 strand for stems and lazy daisy leaves

Madeira cream stranded cotton for French knots dotted around to resemble gypsophila

METHOD

Firstly sew lace table cloth in place at bottom of material leaving approximately 8 cm (3″) of material at bottom.

Paint the white tulle with gold fabric paint and allow to dry. Cut tulle in shape shown on front cover and stitch in place on centre of lace cloth.

Thread gold bullion thread onto large chenille needle and work long criss-cross stitches over tulle on vase as shown.

Using burnt gold braid stitch around edge of tulle over gold thread. Sew outer gold braid around edge twisting the top edges to form a circle on each side of vase and a place to sew old buttons. Sew tassels either side under braid.

Stitch or glue apricot beads and crystals in place, and filigree corners at base of vase. Glue brooch in centre of vase with a strong tacky glue once you have completed flowers to prevent work from becoming too cumbersome.

Make 4 tea roses in colours shown and stitch in place. Make 5 ribbon roses in colours shown and stitch in place. Make 11 smaller ribbon roses and stitch side on to resemble rose buds.

Using green rayon ribbon and Mokuba organza ribbon embroider reverse ribbon leaves and straight stitch leaves on buds where shown.

Embroider pink and gold sprayed flowers and lilacs as discussed in materials.

Embroider reverse ribbon leaves around top in Mokuba green organza ribbon, and 1 strand of DMC 733 for stems.

Scatter French knots around as shown.

I have chosen a very rich burnished silver and gold frame to enhance the colours in the vase.

CREAM BASKET

The roses in this basket are reminiscent of the hybrid musk rose 'Prosperity'. Old ribbons have been combined with new in this simple, but beautiful, basket of flowers. If you are unable to find suitable old ribbons, substitute with the wonderful new variety now available through the stockist section. In any case, the result will be the same.

MATERIALS

Ribbons as listed in glossary
50 cm x 50 cm (20″ x 20″) rich cream damask
Gold mesh material — small piece comes on
  roll
2 gold tassel buttons
4 pearl beads
Glista Birch gold thread
Small suitable piece material for inside basket
Wadding for padding basket

METHOD

Trace basket template onto fabric and stitch gold mesh basket in place, cutting it to fit around edge of template. Slide suitable fabric inside basket, folding edges under and stitching in place. Gently fill basket with wadding to suitable thickness and stitch along top to hold in place.

Stitch gold cord around edge of basket to neaten. Fill basket with soft cream flowers, as shown, using Glista thread to join rayon leaves to flowers.

When finished add tassel buttons for a delightful result.

RIBBON GLOSSARY

Choose contrasting cream ribbons with a slight variation in colour
1 m (1¼ yd) cream grosgrain ribbon 40 mm (1½″) wide
2 m (2½ yd) cream grosgrain ribbon 22 mm (⅞″) wide
2 m (2½ yd) cream rayon ribbon 15 mm (¾″) wide
2 m (2½ yd) cream single-sided satin ribbon 10 mm (½″) wide
3 m (3⅓ yd) white rayon ribbon 10 mm (½″) wide
2 m (2½ yd) cream pure silk ribbon 7 mm (¼″) wide
2 m (2½ yd) cream Mokuba satin-edged ribbon 15 mm (¾″) wide
5 m (5⅓ yd) gold rayon ribbon 10 mm (½″) wide
1 m (1¼ yd) pure silk ribbon 7 mm (¼″) wide col. no. 161
1 m (1¼ yd) gold cord
50 cm (20″) gold mesh (stretchy) for basket

SOFT PASTEL VASE

MATERIALS

Ribbons as listed in glossary

(Again I have used old and new ribbons but you can achieve desired effect by using all new materials.)

50 cm x 50 xm (20" x 20") soft lavender moiré taffeta

DMC 733 2 strands for stems

(L.A. Walsh Oakland C.A. hand-dyed silk thread 1 strand for bullion buds)

DMC 778 3 strands

Gold braid

Two gold metal filigree motifs to decorate vase

Setacolour gold paint

Glista Birch gold thread

2 m (2½ yd) lime green grosgrain ribbon 20 mm (⅞") wide

2 m (2½ yd) Mokuba dusky pink flimsy satin-edged ribbon 15 mm (¾") wide

3 m (3⅓ yd) green rayon ribbon 20 mm (⅞") wide

1 m (1¼ yd) Mokuba dusky pink stiff satin-edged ribbon 15 mm (¾") wide

4 m (4⅓ yd) 7 mm (¼") pure silk ribbon col. 143

4 m (4⅓ yd) 7 mm (¼") pure silk ribbon col. 101

1 m (1¼ yd) Mokuba gold single-sided satin ribbon 15 mm (¾") wide

1 m (1¼ yd) Mokuba satin-edged flimsy gold ribbon 25 mm (1") wide

2 m (2½ yd) gold cord

METHOD

Copy template onto fabric and paint gold as shown.

Using gold braid sew around edge of vase twice.

Embroider Glista thread in straight stitch to form feet of vase. Fill vase with tea and ribbon roses, buds and leaves using ribbons as detailed in glossary.

Attach filigree motifs.

RIBBON GLOSSARY

3 m (3⅓ yd) single-sided satin ribbon dusky pink, 36 mm (1¼") wide

3 m (3⅓ yd) dusky pink matt ribbon, 20 mm (⅞") wide

GOLD BASKET OF FLOPPY GALLICA ROSES

MATERIALS

33 cm x 33 cm (13¼" x 13¼") palest pink Thai silk

3 m (3⅓ yd) pale pink double-sided satin ribbon, 2.5 cm (1") wide

2 m (2½ yd) Mokuba dusky pink satin-edged ribbon, 1.5 cm (¾") wide

1 m (1¼ yd) Mokuba cream satin-edged ribbon, 1.5 cm (¾") wide

50 cm (20") dusky pink double-sided satin ribbon, 2.5 cm (1") wide

1.5 cm (¾") green rayon ribbon, ½ cm (¼") wide

2 m (2½ yd) Mokuba green organza ribbon with gold stripe, ½ cm (¼") wide

2 m (2½ yd) pure silk 4 mm wide ribbon col. no. 170 ½ cm (¼") wide

1 m (1¼ yd) pure silk ribbon col. no. 162 7 mm (¼") wide

3 m (3⅓ yd) variegated chenille thread

Madeira cotton

DMC 3012 Green

DMC 770 Pink 2 strands to make lavender

DMC 640 Grey 2 strands

Glista gold thread

1 m (1¼ yd) gold lamé ribbon, 4 mm (¼") wide

1 m (1¼ yd) contrasting gold thread or braid, 4 mm (¼") wide

50 cm (20") green/gold trimming for edge of basket

50 cm (20") gold lamé ribbon, 2 cm (¾") wide

METHOD

Draw basket on fabric using light-coloured chalk. Cut 14 lengths of gold lamé ribbon to fit horizontally across basket, leaving 1 cm (½″) each side of basket edge, sew into place along basket edge on both sides. Cut contrasting ribbon strips, approximately 13, leaving 1 cm (½″) each end and weave these through horizontally-sewn lamé, to form basket. Sew top and bottom in place along basket line, leaving 1 cm (½″) each side.

Using 2 cm (¾″) gold lamé ribbon, place it under 1 cm (½″) edge and sew down across edge all around basket. Fold lamé over 1 cm (½″) edge and sew neatly around basket to hide selvedge.

Sew green trimming around basket edge and, using Glista gold thread, embroider straight stitch feet at base, in two half-circles.

Make 4 floppy tea roses as shown in stitch glossary using colours shown. Make 6 smaller roses in colours shown and stitch these all in place. Using rayon ribbon and organza ribbon, embroider reverse ribbon leaves around roses, alternating the colours of the leaves as shown.

Using chenille thread and pure silk ribbon no. 162, embroider straight stitch buds. Embroider straight stitch leaves on either side of buds in pure silk col. no. 170. Finish by combining DMC colours for lavender and, using bullion stitch, embroider lavender. DMC 3012 1 strand is used for straight stitch stems and lazy daisy leaves. Scatter French knots in Madeira cotton around basket.

WOVEN BASKET FILLED WITH FLOWERS

MATERIALS

Small piece cream moiré taffeta
DMC 301 Tan for basket
DMC 1078 Gold for basket
All pure silk ribbon is 4 mm (¼″) wide unless
   otherwise stated
2 m (2½ yd) white Birch pure silk ribbon col.
   3 for gypsophila
4 m (4⅓ yd) pink Birch pure silk ribbon col.
   157 for rosettes
4 m (4⅓ yd) plum Birch pure silk ribbon col.
   159 for buds
2 m (2½ yd) yellow Birch pure silk ribbon col.
   15 for wheat
2 m (2½ yd) purple Birch pure silk ribbon col.
   179 for wisteria
DMC 819 Pale pink straight stitch buds 2 strands
DMC 326 Red grub buds 2 strands
DMC 3042 Mauve grub wisteria 2 strands
DMC 3364 Green
DMC 524 Light green
DMC 676 Beige

METHOD

Draw basket template on fabric.

Using gold thread, work stem stitch around basket edge. Still using gold make long horizontal straight stitches from one end of basket to the other, filling in basket.

Then repeat vertically. Using DMC 301 tan 2 strands, weave under and over between gold stitches both horizontally and vertically to give basket effect.

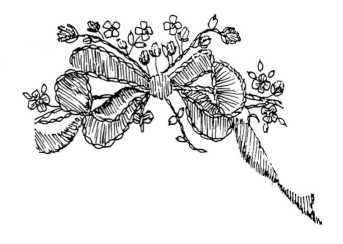

Using gold thread, work satin stitch to form small feet at base of basket.

Fill basket with flowers, as shown in stitch glossary.

SMALL BLUE BASKET

MATERIALS

20 cm x 30 cm (8″ x 12″) blue moiré taffeta

1 m (1¼ yd) pale blue double-sided satin ribbon, 5 mm (2″) wide

Pure silk ribbon all 4 mm (¼″) wide: Pale blue col. 44, Green col. 33, Pink col. 163, Light green col. 62, Dark green col. 72

DMC Colours: 334 Blue, 367 Green stem 1 strand, 676 Yellow, 340 Lilac, 211 Pale lilac, 208 Purple, Ecru, 834 Mustard wattle, 224 Musk, pink buds, Pink, buds

Au ver à soie S.A. metallic thread col. 048 — Mauve

Glista Birch gold thread

METHOD

Copy template onto fabric and, using stem stitch, embroider around edge and diagonally across vase as shown, filling in feet at base of vase with straight stitches.

Fill the vase using colours as shown.

VIOLETS

MATERIALS

50 cm x 50 cm (20″ x 20″) rich golden silk dupion

5 m (5⅓ yd) pure silk ribbon col. 84, 4 mm (¼″) wide

5 m (5⅓ yd) pure silk ribbon col. 21 dark green, 4 mm (¼″) wide

5 m (5⅓ yd) pure silk ribbon col. 20 lighter green 4 mm (¼″) wide

DMC 444 3 strands for French knot centre

DMC 550 2 strands for shadow around violets

DMC 520 2 strands Green for stems and around leaves

DMC 320 2 strands Green for stems and around leaves

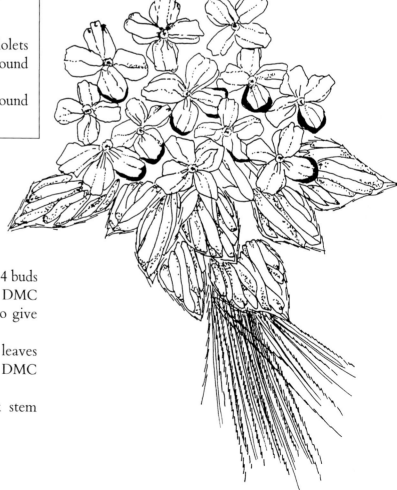

METHOD

Using col. 84 work violets as shown, making 4 buds to form violet. Embroider French knot centre DMC 444 and outline edge of some violet petals to give shadowed effect with 2 strands DMC 550.

Using alternate shades of green, work leaves in long and short straight stitches and outline DMC greens.

Using DMC 520 and DMC 320, work stem stitch stems 2 strands.

ORGANZA BASKET FILLED WITH POLYANTHA ROSES:FAIRY, CECILE BRUNNER AND PURPLE BABY FAURA

MATERIALS

2 m (2½ yd) pale mauve organza

½ m (20″) soft pink bem silk lining

2 m (2½ yd) soft pale pink double-sided satin ribbon, 2 cm (¾″) wide

½ m (20″) deeper pink single-sided satin ribbon, 2 cm (¾″) wide for roses

½ m (20″) soft lavender double-sided satin ribbon, 2 cm (¾″) wide

1 m (1¼ yd) soft green double-sided satin ribbon, 5 mm (2″) wide for leaves

1 m (1¼ yd) mauve sheer rayon ribbon for buds

1 m (1¼ yd) purple organza ribbon, 30 mm wide

½ m (20″) single-sided satin ribbon, dusky pink for tea rose, 35 mm (1¼″) wide

DMC 778 Pink 2 strands for straight stitch buds

Madeira 0815 silk 2 strands for grub buds

Pure silk ribbon col. 22 for buds, 4 mm (⅛″) wide

DMC 524 1 strand for fly stitch and lazy daisy leaves

DMC 210 2 strands for bullion wisteria

2 m (2½ yd) pure silk 7 mm (¼″) col. 73 for straight stitch leaves on large ribbon buds

5 mm 1 m wide dark green shot with burgundy rayon ribbon for leaves

DMC 3042 2 strands for grapes

1 m lavender 1 cm seam binding or equivalent (not satin but matt)

For basket: Au ver à soie col. 012 Balger 1 strand, DMC 3041 1 strand

METHOD

Cut 25 cm x 25 cm (10″ x 10″) organza (cushion measures 18 cm x 18 cm (7″ x 7″) without frill when made up).

Work basket with 1 strand DMC alternated with 1 strand of the Au ver à soie in shadow stitch. Make up ribbon and tea roses and stitch in place. Embroider small buds etc., as shown. To finish design, embroider small cluster at base of basket.

Cushion is made with a 15 cm frill pleated by a specialist pleating service available through the Yellow Pages.

Small blue basket

Spring flower spray

Woven basket filled with flowers

Violets

Organza basket filled with polyantha roses: Fairy, Cecile Brunner and purple baby faura

LAVENDER CUSHION

MATERIALS

50 cm (20″) green silk or moiré taffeta

50 cm (20″) mauve silk or moiré taffeta for ruche

DMC Colours: 3041 Dark mauve, 3042 Light mauve, 542 Green (mixed to make lavender), 208 Deep purple, 3041 Dark mauve, 3364 Green (mixed to make contrasting lavender)

METHOD

Cut green fabric 35 cm x 37 cm (14″ x 14½″) (when made up 32 cm x 34 cm) (12½″ x 13″)

This lavender cushion is simply superb and actually looks like a bunch of lavender placed onto a pillow. To achieve the rich quality of the lavender, three DMC colours are mixed. I find it useful to first rule a straight line in very light pencil on your fabric where you wish to place your lavender. It is a good idea to have a central point where you will place a bow after completing your cushion.

Alternative colours to use for a deeper colour: DMC 550 Dark purple, 553 Mid purple, 367 Green (2 strands of each mixed together) 553 Mid purple, 211 Pale purple, 367 Green (2 strands of each mixed together) 550 Dark purple, 3042 Light mauve, 367 Green (2 strands of each mixed together)

Start at the top of each pencilled line and work in bullion stitch for lavender heads. Stems are made by working stem stitch from base of lavender head to end of pencilled line. Place a ribbon bow in your choice of colour in centre of bunch.

BRIDAL AND BABY EMBROIDERY

SATIN HEART CUSHION
WITH ANTIQUE TASSEL

MATERIALS

1.5 m (1⅓ yd) cream damask
2 m (2½ yd) thick cord for inside ruche
3 m (3⅓ yd) cream braid
5 m (5⅓ yd) double-sided satin ribbon, 22 mm (⅞″) wide
Complementary braid and tassel

METHOD

Cut fabric in a heartshape, about 34 cm wide x 34 cm (13″ x 13″) from base of heart to centre top.

Draw heart template in centre and make about 40 roses to sew in centre of heart.

Sew cream braid around roses and attach interesting tassel on top of braid.

Make cushion up with ruche and sew extra cream braid around edge.

WEDDING RING CUSHION

MATERIALS

1 m (1¼ yd) cream damask/moiré/Thai silk

50 cm (20″) interesting gold braid (I have used an Indian braid with small pearls.)

50 cm (20″) flimsy gold-edged ribbon 1 cm (½″) wide for bow

2 m (2½ yd) pure silk ribbon 7 mm (¼″) wide col. 162, for small ribbon roses

DMC 647 1 strand for lazy daisy leaves

DMC 644 1 strand for fly stitch around buds

Madeira pure silk thread col. 0815 1 strand for grub buds

Madeira stranded cotton white (on reel) for straight stitch buds and French knots

Glista Birch thread for small French knots and grub buds, and stem stitch initials

1 gold Cherub (painted with gold paint) as for gold-painted Cupid cushion

METHOD

Cut 28 cm x 31 cm (11″ x 12½″) piece of chosen fabric (when finished cushion front will measure 25 cm x 28 cm [10″ x 11″]).

Cut gold braid in half and make 2 hearts. Stitch in place on fabric, 2 cm (¾″) apart.

Thread flimsy gold-edged ribbon through wide-eyed chenille needle and make a looped bow by bringing ribbon through fabric and down again next to first hole, repeating on other side and working one straight stitch in centre of bow. Bring ribbon up at centre of bow and through fabric again a little way down to form tails of bow. Stitch down to hold bow in place.

Sew painted cherub above bow and using 1 strand of DMC 644, embroider stem stitch as shown in picture. Embroider grub buds with 1 strand of 0815 Madeira silk thread and Glista French knots. With pure silk ribbon col. 162, make 5 small ribbon roses and sew in place as shown. Embroider Glista grub buds around roses, lazy daisy leaves and French knots in Madeira stranded cotton.

To finish work, using 1 strand Glista gold thread, embroider in stem stitch initials of the bride and groom.

WEDDING HORSESHOE

MATERIALS

2 strips silk fabric, 2.5 cm (2″) wide x 1 m (1¼ yd)

1 m (1¼ yd) cream double-sided satin ribbon, 15 mm (¾″) wide

1 cardboard horseshoe

2 m (2½ yd) cream satin-edged Mokuba ribbon, 10 mm (½″) wide

1 m gold metallic Mokuba ribbon, 10 mm (½″) wide

Extra ribbon

METHOD

Sew silk strips right sides together and finish by sewing one end together and then turn right side out. Push material over horseshoe (make sure you use very stiff cardboard) until gathered evenly. Sew end of horseshoe at inside bottom edge. Make 1 cream tea rose in satin-edged ribbon and stitch to centre of horseshoe. Make 2 cream double-sided satin ribbon roses and attach as shown. Make 2 satin-edged roses placing them as in picture, and attach ribbon leaves as shown. Attach ribbon length to back of horseshoe in a bow and sew securely.

GARDENIA WEDDING RING CUSHION

MATERIALS

1.5 m (1⅔ yd) wedding dress material

3 hanks of DMC Ecru

3 m (3⅓ yd) cream double-sided satin ribbon,
   15 mm (6″) wide

5 m (5⅓ yd) Birch pure silk ribbon white, 4 mm
   (⅛″) wide

1 pkt Madeira silk thread white

DMC 368

3 m (3⅓ yd) Birch pure silk ribbon col. 154,
   4 mm (⅛″) wide

METHOD

Cut 30 cm x 32 cm (12″ x 12½″) square of wedding dress fabric (leaving extra for seam allowance).

Draw oval template on centre fabric and, using 1 strand DMC 368, work in stem stitch around oval. Draw bow from template and, using 4 strands of DMC Ecru, complete bow in satin stitch.

Make 3 gardenias as shown in stitch glossary and sew securely in place. Embroider buds around gardenias in white silk and DMC Ecru as shown. DMC buds are worked in 3 strands and silk buds are worked by sewing 3 straight stitches.

Buds at either side of gardenia are worked by combining silk ribbon straight stitches with Madeira straight stitches (2 strands) either side. Using 1 strand of DMC 368 attach buds to gardenias using fly stitch. Embroider buds around bow as shown.

Using 1 strand DMC Ecru, embroider initials of bride and groom in stem and satin stitch. Finish off by embroidering heart in long straight stitches in Ecru 2 strands.

Make up cushion with 4 cm (1½″) ruche and pipe in same fabric.

WEDDING DRESS DETAIL

Whatever the style of wedding dress, you can still enhance the design and even make a stunning feature of large soft ribbon roses. I have used my own wedding dress to show how effective and easy it is to add a final touch.

You can add these roses to the neckline or shoulders, or in the centre of a large bow at the back of your dress — it is really up to your imagination as to where you would like to place them.

MATERIALS

2 m (2½ yd) white double-sided satin ribbon, 50 mm (2″) wide

1.5 m (1⅔ yd) sheer silver-edged metallic ribbon, 35 mm (1¼″) wide

1.5 m (1⅔ yd) sheer gold-edged metallic Makuba ribbon, 35 mm (1¼″) wide

4 m (4⅓ yd) sheer gold metallic Makuba silk ribbon

METHOD

Using white double-sided satin ribbon make 2 large floppy tea roses with petals as shown.

Using silver metallic ribbon make 2 roses with petals as shown.

Using gold-edged metallic ribbon make 3 smaller roses, without petals.

Stitch all roses in desired place. Using gold metallic ribbon make separate leaves and stitch in place around roses, as shown on dress.

Top Right: **Wedding ring cushion**
Top Left: **Gold painted cupid cushion**
Middle: **Gardenia wedding ring cushion**
Bottom: **Satin heart cushion with antique tassel**

Wedding dress with two horseshoes

Forget-me-not baby pillow with baby blanket

ORGET-ME-NOT AND ROSEBUD BABY FRAME

MATERIALS

28 cm x 26 cm (11″ x 10½″) white moiré taffeta or equivalent

DMC Colours: White, 775 Pale blue, 819 Pale pink, 524 Pale green, 3022 Moss green, 746 Pale lemon

METHOD

Draw oval and bow template onto fabric and, working with 3 strands of DMC White, embroider in stem stitch very closely around oval. Again with 3 strands of DMC White, fill in bow with satin stitch. When completed use 1 strand of White to outline bow in neat stem stitch.

With 2 strands of DMC 524 and working in stem stitch, create a vine effect around oval and above and below bow. Using 1 strand of DMC 775 work very delicate forget-me-nots (lazy daisy stitch) all around vine as shown and embroidering lazy daisy leaves with 1 strand of 524.

With 1 strand of 819, embroider grub buds (16 wraps) around vine attaching them to vine with 1 strand of 5022 in fly stitch. Using 1 strand lemon, work French knots in centre of forget-me-not. Embroider 'Baby' in centre in satin stitch, using either DMC 746 lemon, DMC 819 pink, or DMC 775 blue as shown.

Frame as you wish.

BABY BLANKET

MATERIALS

1 bassinet-size baby blanket in pure new wool

50 cm (20") cream double-sided satin ribbon, 10 mm (½") wide

50 cm (20") pink double-sided satin ribbon, 10 mm (½") wide

Paternayan Wools: 262 Cream, 755 Lemon, 923 Rose middle, 964 Pink outer (star flower), Pale pink, 344 Mauve — bow and grapes and star flower

DMC Colours: 819 Pale pink, 746 Pale lemon, 211 Light mauve French knots, 775 Pale blue, 3042 Bullions, 3364 Green, 676 Beige

Madeira turquoise

METHOD

Draw heart and bow template on blanket. Make 3 cream ribbon roses and 2 pink ones and sew securely in place as shown on heart.

Using 1 strand DMC 3364 embroider leaves and stems on flowers, as shown. Using 1 strand 344 wool embroider bow in satin stitch above heart.

Using Lemon 755 and DMC 676 for French knot as centre, work a lazy daisy on either side of rose. Continue on heart template line and embroider grub rose in wool using 1 strand, star flowers, buds, etc. finishing at base of heart point with 3 lemon French knots.

FORGET-ME-NOT BABY PILLOW

By embroidering the baby's name instead of 'Baby' the pillow becomes personalised.

MATERIALS

1.5 m (1⅔ yd) soft white washable fabric (lawn or damask)

DMC Colours: 775 Pale blue, 746 Pale lemon, 819 Pale pink, 524 Green, White.

Crewel needle no. 6.

METHOD

Cut out 36 cm x 36 cm (14½″ x 14½″) square of fabric, leaving 2 cm (¼″) for seam allowance. Draw bow and oval template onto fabric and embroider bow in satin stitch using 3 strands of DMC White.

Using 1 strand of DMC 524 embroider stem stitch around oval. With 2 strands of DMC 775 pale blue, embroider small forget-me-nots (lazy daisy stitch) around oval, filling in centre with a French knot in 2 strands of DMC 746.

Embroider lazy daisy leaves in 1 strand of DMC 524 around forget-me-nots. With 2 strands of DMC 819, work grub buds in as shown and joining them with 'Y' stitch in DMC 524. 1 strand embroider 'Baby' in satin stitch (2 strands) including bud as shown. See note.

You can work triangles of forget-me-nots and buds as shown in the corners of the cushion.

Note: You can work 'Baby' in lemon, or pink or blue.

BABY

GOLD-PAINTED CUPID CUSHION

MATERIALS

1.5 m (1⅔ yd) cream damask
1 gold cupid
2 m (2½ yd) double-sided cream satin ribbon,
   22 mm (⅞″) wide
2 m (2½ yd) Mokuba soft, sheer, cream satin-
   edged ribbon, 15 mm (¾″) wide
Birch Glista gold metallic thread
DMC Ecru
Birch pure silk ribbon, col. 4 mm wide
1.5 m (1⅔ yd) cord for ruche

METHOD

Draw template onto fabric and stitch roses in place. Using Glista thread, shape leaves in straight stitches as shown and bullion buds along stems, joining cream roses.

At top of design use Glista thread and embroider bullion buds with lazy daisy stitch around them to give unusual effect.

Using 2 strands, embroider buds in Ecru and silk ribbon buds where shown, using Glista thread in fly stitch to join them to roses.

You will notice a black coating around the gold Cupid; to give the Cupid a more antique appearance soak it in mineral turpentine for an hour or so, then brush with a toothbrush — the black coating will disappear. Brush Cupid with vinegar as this acts as a base for the paint. Paint Cupid with Duncan Decorator Acrylics solid gold colour paint and leave to dry overnight. Using Glista thread, sew Cupid in place.

 # TRINKET EMBROIDERY

 # PALE BLUE LADY

MATERIALS

1 silk picture of lady

27 cm x 27 cm (10¾" x 10¾") ice blue Thai
  silk

1 m (1¼ yd) white pretty lace edging

1 m (1¼ yd) blue and white embroidered
  trimming

1 m (1¼ yd) strand small pearls

DMC 948 — outer grub rose 1 strand

760 — centre of grub roses 1 strand

3731 — buds 1 strand

934 — 1 strand for stems

Birch Glista gold thread

5 extra pearls

Pure silk pale blue ribbon col. 44, 13 mm (¾")
  wide

METHOD

Using fray stopper around edge of picture, sew
photo of lady onto centre of fabric. Lay embroidered trimming around photo, folding the corners
neatly so that the pattern runs evenly around
picture. Work in the same manner with lace. Using
1 strand of DMC colours, embroider bullion roses
in place as shown. Sew pearls and embroider gold
lazy daisy leaves as shown.

Thread pure silk ribbon through large-eye
chenille needle and pull through fabric to make
small bows in each corner.

Stitch pearls around edge of photo to complete
work.

Gilded bow heart and cherub

Lavender cushion

Pink lady

Pale blue lady

PINK LADY

MATERIALS

1 silk picture of lady

27 cm x 27 cm (10¾″ x 10¾″) soft pink Thai silk

1 m (1¼ yd) soft pink ribbon (I used seam binding 22 mm [⅞″] wide)

1 m (1¼ yd) pink cording

Birch Glista gold thread

3 small pearls

3 small pink beads

DMC 948 1 strand for bullion buds

METHOD

Use fray stopper around edge of Thai silk and silk picture. Sew pearls, beads and Glista thread as shown on picture and embroider bullion buds. Secure picture to material and fold pink ribbon around edge and stitch into place. Make a bow and sew at top of work. Stitch cord in place around ribbon to finish off.

GREEN FAIRY

MATERIALS

28 cm x 32 cm (11″ x 12½″) pale green Thai silk

1 bread dough fairy piece

4 m (4⅓ yd) pure silk ribbon, col. 162 7 mm (¼″) wide for bows and 6 roses

2 m (2½ yd) pure silk ribbon, col. 143 7 mm (¼″) wide for 4 gold roses

DMC 648 Green 1 strand around circle

DMC 832 3 strands for French knots 2 wraps

DMC 3022 1 strand for lazy daisy stitch leaves

DMC 676 2 strands for yellow daisy and centre of pink daisy and wattle

I have used a dusky pink pure silk Oakland C.A. thread for pink daisies — substitute 1 strand Anchor linen thread col. L5400 or DMC 224

50 cm (20″) Mokuba satin-edged flimsy dusky pink ribbon

DMC Pearl green thread for larger lazy daisy leaves

No 3 Birch Glista thread for lazy daisy leaves and grub buds

METHOD

Draw circle template on fabric and work in 1 strand of DMC 648 in stem stitch around edge. In middle of circle at bottom edge make a small looped bow (see stitch glossary). Make 3 ribbon roses with Mokuba ribbon and stitch base of circle as shown and embroider other flower and leaves in place.

With 3 strands of 832, work French knots evenly around the circle. Glue on bread dough piece using tacky glue, as discussed in Gilded Bow Heart and Cherub instructions, see pages 60–1, and embroider looped bow at base of feet.

GILDED BOW HEART AND CHERUB

MATERIALS

35 cm x 35 cm (14″ x 14″) bridal white Thai silk

2 plastic 'Jinkets' (gilded by Elizabeth Garratt)

5 m (16 ft) pure silk ribbon col. no. 162, 7 mm (¼″) wide

DMC 647 1 strand lazy daisy leaves

2 m (2½ yd) white pure silk ribbon, 4 mm (¼″) wide

Madeira silk thread 0815 for pink buds with white Madeira cotton straight stitch either side

DMC 3743 Lavender 1 strand, 20 wraps

DMC 676 Wattle 2 strands, 1 wrap

Birch Glista gold thread for bullion buds, 10 wraps

Note: I have used old gold thread (unavailable) for French knots in between outer ribbon heart. Substitute Glista 2 strands and 5 wraps for French knots.

METHOD

Draw heart template onto fabric and using pure silk ribbon col. 162, embroider small straight stitches all the way around edge taking care to keep ribbon flat. Using Glista 2 strands work French knots in between straight stitches.

Using Glista 1 strand embroider stem stitch around central smaller heart. Sew twirled ribbon roses onto stem stitch heart as shown, leaving slight gap at the top. Embroider remaining flowers in place as shown. Glue gilded pieces in position using a good tacky glue. (I have used Aleene's Designer Tacky Glue. You will notice when using this that it is stark white when brushed on your piece but it will dry clear.)

Lay work flat and allow to dry overnight.

ARROW FAIRY

MATERIALS

1 small bread dough fairy

25 cm x 27 cm (10″ x 10⅝″) cream damask

50 cm (20″) apricot rayon ribbon, 1 cm (½″) wide

50 cm (20″) pure silk ribbon col. 162, 7 mm (¼″) wide

2 m (2½ yd) pure silk ribbon col. 111, 4 mm

DMC 760 Deep apricot 1 strand, grub bud

DMC 3743 mauve grub with Madeira stranded cotton 1514 either side

DMC 648 Green 1 strand

Gold bullion

Pure silk ribbon col. 74

Small length fine gold cord

METHOD

Glue fairy in place with tacky glue. (Refer to instructions for Gilded Bow Heart and Cherub, see pages 60–1.) This piece will not be difficult to work around as it is very light. It is best to position the fairy first so you can design your work around it.

Once fairy is glued, make up ribbon roses in colours shown and secure in place. Embroider other stitches as shown and embroider straight stitch pure silk leaves col. 74 around roses.

Using gold bullion coils, stretch out in parts and catch sections down with tiny stitches using Glista thread. Leave some ends of bullion coiled up to give glittered effect.

Tie a small bow and stitch in place at bottom of work.

DOVE FAIRY

MATERIALS

25 cm x 25 cm (10″ x 10″) ice blue Thai silk
1 small bread dough fairy with doves
50 cm (20″) pure silk ribbon col. 44 pale blue
    7 mm (¼″) wide, for central flower (I have
    used an American ribbon which is unavail-
    able here)
50 cm (20″) palest green double-sided satin
    ribbon for large ribbon leaves, 5 mm (2″)
    wide
1 m (1¼ yd) pure silk ribbon col. 162 7 mm
    (¼″) wide, for 4 ribbon roses
3 m (3¾ yd) pure silk ribbon col. 74 4 mm (⅛″)
    wide for bow and small ribbon leaves
Glista thread for lazy daisy leaves
DMC Colours: 3747 forget-me-nots 2 strands,
    834 for wattle and centre of forget-me-nots
    2 strands
733 for brighter lazy daisy leaves 1 strand
644 for light lazy daisy leaves around forget-
    me-nots and extra leaves on sprays 1 strand
778 for grub buds 1 strand joined by 644 fly
    stitches

METHOD

Glue bread dough piece onto fabric with tacky
glue. 2.5 cm (1″) below foot, embroider a small
blue daisy in looped bow stitch to make small
petals. Place 3 French knots in DMC 834 2 strands
in centre of flower. Make four pure silk ribbon
roses and sew two larger ones either side of central
blue flower. Embroider other flowers and satin
ribbon leaves around flower, finishing cluster with
1 lazy daisy leaf in Glista thread at both ends.

Using 1 strand of DMC 733 and working in stem stitch, embroider a vine sloping out both sides from fairy piece. This is a guide on which you embroider the flowers, as if they are a continuation of the flowers in the dough piece. Embroider flowers as shown to make a small looped bow with pure silk ribbon, and embroider a few Glista straight stitches at the top to give a sheen.

Top left and right: **Dove fairy and arrow fairy**
Bottom left and right: **Fairy in love and green fairy**

Top: Gold cushion with 1950s' braid
Middle right: Bourbon rose–La Reine Victoria cushion
Bottom: Soft blue scallopped cushion

GLENYS RICHARDS

VALERIE FERGUSON

DEBRA HOLLAND

MELISSA SMITH

LOUISE DONNE

JENNY BRADD

The pieces displayed above are examples of students' work: there are no instructions for these projects in the book.

FAIRY IN LOVE

MATERIALS

23 cm x 23 cm (9″ x 9″) piece pale green Thai silk

1 bread dough fairy piece

4 m (4⅓ yd) pure silk ribbon col. 162 7 mm (¼″) wide

2.5 m (2⅔yd) pure silk ribbon col. 111 7 mm (¼″) wide

DMC 648 for vine 1 strand

DMC 524 for fly stitch and lazy daisy leaves

DMC 778 for grub buds 1 strand

Madeira silk col. 0815 1 strand for straight stitch buds

1.5 m (1⅔ yd) pure silk ribbon 4 mm (⅛″) wide col. 74

METHOD

Glue fairy 8 cm (3″) from top of fabric with tacky glue and trace heart shape beneath fairy.

Thread 162 pure silk ribbon through large chenille needle and make looped bow at base of heart. Bring needle through material at edge of bow and twist to form spiral effect going up heart to fairy and stitch in place. Using DMC 648 1 strand embroider in stem stitch around ribbon to give a vine effect.

Make up tiny ribbon roses in alternating pure silk colours 162 and 111 as shown, and stitch them in position carefully. Using pure silk ribbon col. 74 embroider straight stitch leaves around large roses as shown.

SENSUOUS OCELOT CUSHION

Not a cushion for the faint of heart.

MATERIALS

50 cm (20″) ocelot fabric — I have used a good
    quality fur fabric
5 m (5½ yd) Mokuba single-sided, black-edged
    red velvet ribbon 38 mm (1½″) wide
2 m (2½ yd) rich red cord
2 m (2½ yd) green rayon ribbon
1 m (1¼ yd) green wire-edged ribbon
DMC green 520 6 strands for stems
1 m (1¼ yd) brown taffeta ribbon 38 mm (1½″)
    wide

METHOD

Cut 42 cm x 42 cm (16¾″ x 16¾″) (39 cm x 39 cm/
15½″ x 15½″ when made up) of ocelot fabric and
make 7 deep red roses and secure in place. Make
3 bud roses and stitch in place also. Using rayon
ribbon threaded through wide-eyed chenille
needle, embroider straight stitch leaves on roses
shown, and large lazy daisy leaves either side of
bottom 2 roses. Using wire-edged ribbon make 5
leaves and stitch in place. Using 6 strands DMC
520 work in stem stitch to make stems. Make a
bow and attach to roses.

    Sew cord around edge of cushion when made up.

SOFT BLUE SCALLOPED CUSHION

MATERIALS

1 m (1¼ yd) ice blue Thai silk

50 cm (20″) white Thai silk

1 m (1¼ yd) white seam binding 25 mm (1″) wide (or substitute white double-sided satin ribbon)

2 m (2½ yd) Birch blue pure silk ribbon col. 125 7 mm (¼″) wide

4 m (4⅓ yd) Birch pale blue silk ribbon col. 124 4mm (⅛″) wide

4 m (4⅓ yd) Birch ice blue silk ribbon col. 124 4mm (⅛″) wide

1 m (1¼ yd) cream ruffle edged braid with blue embroidered detail

Madeira white stranded cotton thread

1 m (1¼ yd) shell pink double-sided satin ribbon 5 mm (¼″) wide

1 m (1¼ yd) green flimsy rayon ribbon

DMC Pale green 524

DMC Moss green 3022

DMC Pale grey 762

Silver bullion thread (or substitute Birch Glista silver thread)

Perle palest green thread

METHOD

Cut 28 cm x 28 cm (11″ x 11″) squares of blue Thai silk leaving 2 cm (¾″) for seam allowance. Draw circle template on centre of fabric. Make up 4 gathered primroses and stitch in place evenly around circle. Make 4 white, blue and shell pink ribbon roses and sew in place evenly around circle as shown.

Using blue silk ribbon col. no. 44, embroider buds out from white roses, attaching them with 1 strand DMC 3022.

Using flimsy rayon ribbon, stitch 4 straight stitch leaves around white roses.

Embroider white cotton buds with 1 strand and 3 straight stitches, attaching them to shell pink roses with 1 strand DMC 524.

Embroider French knot grapes in DMC 762 3 strands as shown and ice blue silk ribbon lazy daisy leaves around shell pink roses.

Finally, add silver bullion buds 1 strand 10 wraps around needle and make a lazy daisy stitch around these. Work silver bullion French knots and the design is completed.

Make up cushion using contrasting colour and scalloped edges.

Bourbon Rose
LA REINE VICTORIA CUSHION

MATERIALS

50 cm (20″) dusky pink moiré taffeta

2 m (2½ yd) Mokuba dusky pink satin-edged ribbon 15 mm (¾″) wide

50 cm (20″) ruched green embroidered ribbon for primroses

1.5 m (1⅔ yd) double-sided satin ribbon dusky pink 10 mm (½″) wide

1 m (1¼ yd) dark green rayon ribbon for large leaves

Madeira stranded cotton apricot col. 1514 for buds and DMC 368 1 strand lazy daisy leaves

1 m (1¼ yd) pure silk ribbon 4 mm (⅛″) wide col. 154 for pale green leaves

DMC 3042 3 strands for grapes with 2 strands of DMC 3012 for leaves and stem

Anchor (MEZ) 090 2 strands for bright pink buds with pure silk 154 leaves either side

DMC mauve 211 for French knots in centre and around edge, and lavender with DMC 368 1 strand for lazy daisy leaves

50 cm (20″) palest pink double-sided satin ribbon 5 mm (¼″) wide for 2 small roses

1 m (1¼ yd) pure silk 7 mm (¼″) ribbon col. 158 for 4 small ribbon roses

2 small pink and green flowers available as a length of braid, cut up and stitched in pairs in between pure silk roses col. 158

suitable fringing and piping

METHOD

Cut 32 cm x 32 cm (12½″ x 12½″) of moiré (when made up measures 30 cm x 32 cm/12″ x 12″). Draw circle template onto fabric and make 4 tea roses as shown in Techniques, using Mokuba satin-edged ribbon. Make 4 ruched green primroses as shown in Techniques and stitch in between tea roses. Make 8 dusky pink ribbon roses and secure in pairs on left-hand side of tea rose. Make 2 palest pink ribbon roses and secure on right side of tea rose. Using green rayon ribbon, work leaves around tea roses. Finish by embroidering other flowers as shown.

SPRING FLOWER SPRAY

This design was created from a bowl of flowers collected from my garden.

MATERIALS

50 cm (20″) mauve ribbon 2.5 cm (1″) wide — for 2 large roses

25 cm (10″) pink seam binding, 2.5 cm (1″) wide

25 cm (10″) pink organza ribbon, 10 mm (½″ wide)

50 cm (20″) white ribbon, 5 cm (½″) wide

1 m (1¼ yd) green ruched embroidered ribbon for primroses

2 m (2½ yd) white pure silk ribbon 3 mm (1⅛″) wide

DMC 209, 3042, 208, for wisteria — 4 strands 320 Green 2 strands for stems and leaves, 208 1 strand for straight stitch spikes and 320 for heads and stems. 3747 2 strands for forget-me-nots, 733 6 strands for wattle French knots

3 m (3⅓ yd) 4 mm (⅛″) pure silk ribbon no. 33 and no. 20 for large straight stitch leaves

1.50 m (1⅔ yd) pure silk ribbon 31 for leaves on white daisies

1.50 m (1⅔ yd) pure silk ribbon 4 mm (⅛″) 158 for buds at top, with DMC 3012 as fly stitch and stems

2 m (2½ yd) 7 mm (¼″) pure silk ribbon col. 73 leaves on wisteria

METHOD

Work all ribbon flowers first and add embroidered hanging flowers last.

WISTERIA LADY

I have been fortunate to find handmade old silk flowers from France still with their labels intact. They are truly a rare find and these two wisteria flowers are an exquisite example. If you do come across old silk flowers they are generally a little flat and worse for wear. To bring them to life you need do no more than hold them a few inches above a steaming kettle and they will transform before your eyes.

The lady I purchased these flowers from was very knowledgeable and also suggested using a vacuum cleaner (head removed) to gently draw them out. She said this was the method she used and that it achieved good results.

MATERIALS

60 cm x 50 cm (24″ x 20″) moiré taffeta
1 silk picture
strand of pearls
1 pearl drop
2 interesting old flowers
1 m (1¼ yd) green organza ribbon 50 mm (2″) wide
1 m (1¼ yd) Mokuba one sided green velvet ribbon 1 cm (½″) wide
2 m (2½ yd) Mokuba flimsy satin edged ribbon pink 1 cm (½″) wide
2 m (2½ yd) Mokuba dark green rayon ribbon 1 cm (½″) wide
9 amethyst crystal beads
13 pearl beads
DMC lime green pearl thread
3 m (3⅓ yd) pure silk ribbon, 4 mm (¼″) wide col. 101 for buds
Mauve chenille thread for buds

> Mokuba green organza ribbon with satin stripe for bow on silk picture and alternate leaves around bow

METHOD

Attach silk picture with tacky glue and sew strand of pearls around edge. Place old flowers, or alternative, to form arched effect around the picture. Using organza wide ribbon, make a bow and stitch around picture to form a halo effect, joining onto old flowers.

Using velvet ribbon, make a smaller bow and a roped entwined effect around organza ribbon, and stitch in place.

Make 2 tea roses and stitch in place as shown. Make 5 small ribbon roses and secure onto design. Embroider buds, ribbon leaves and stems as shown. Finally, sew crystal beads and pearls in place and attach bow to top of silk picture and pearl drop at base.

STUDENTS' SECTION

One of the nice elements that has come from teaching embroidery is the friendships made along the way. The pleasure of the classes, as much for the students as myself, flows from these friendships as well as from the embroidery itself. I feel privileged to be doing something for which I have a passion while gaining friends.

Each design from my students is an individual and beautiful example of skills learnt in class, combined with their own techniques. I learn as much from them in the process.

GLENYS RICHARDS

GOLD CUPID

Glenys' work is her signature — she has a beautiful technique that is hers alone. This embroidered cherub is an example of fine gold bullion work blended in delicate detail with the finest embroidery and dainty pearls.

VALERIE FERGUSON

Val's intricate embroidery is always a labour of love. She is meticulous with each stitch and what starts as a small and simple project, finishes as an elaborate creation. Val embroidered this superb initial in memory of her grandmother, Daisy Lillian Babbage (my great grandmother). Embroidery does run in the family!

DEBRA HOLLAND

Debra's piece is exceptional in its design. Her designs are whimsical, always have a sense of fun

and are very individual. She always delights me
with her new ideas and creativity.

MELISSA SMITH

Melissa's baby quilt is a stunning example of fine
embroidery combined with larger ribbon roses.
Melissa has combined wool, silk threads and
ribbons, Madeira stranded cotton and cording to
create this beautiful piece. The bows have been
appliquéd onto the fabric and striped piping used
to complement the design. Any baby would look
divine snuggled under this.

LOUISE DONNE

Louise has used a striking contrast of fabric and
threads to achieve a simple, but stunning piece of
embroidery. This particular design would be easy
and ideal for a beginner as there are only a few
simple stitches used, but because of the dramatic
colours chosen, the end result looks very advanced.
The large gold cupid adds a touch of elegance..

JENNY BRADD

Jenny is one of the younger members of the class,
joining when she was 19. Her original design is
a terrific idea for either a 21st, 18th or whatever
milestone you wish to remember. She designed this
piece for her own 21st. This is a beautiful way
to recall the occasion, with each guest signing the
mattboard.

Another design would be to make ribbon roses
and small buds and grub roses into the numerals
to give a more three-dimensional look, and have
it framed in an object box. This type of design
makes a beautiful and everlasting gift.

TECHNIQUES

HOW TO MAKE THE ROSE

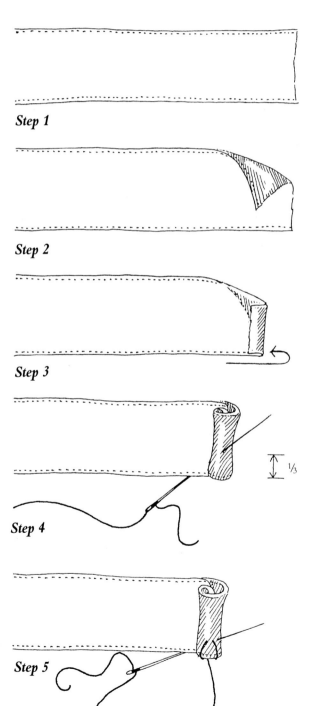

Fold edge of ribbon over at corner.

Roll end of ribbon several times to cover folded edge.

Stitch securely ⅓ of way up roll.

Stitch several times to ensure coil does not unfold.

Step 1

Step 2

Step 3

Step 4

Step 5

Turn top of ribbon away from roll as shown.

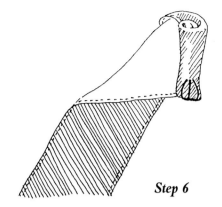

Step 6

Roll central roll toward turned away ribbon (to left) and stitch left side and base securely.

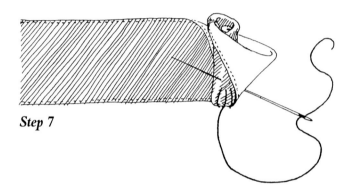

Step 7

Stitch right side and base several times. This will ensure rose will not fall apart.

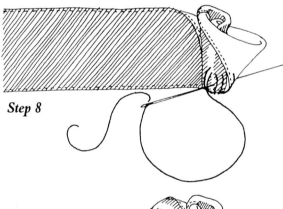

Step 8

Turn left ribbon length away from central bud, as above.

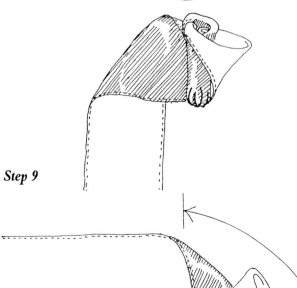

Step 9

Roll ribbon bud onto folded length.

Step 10

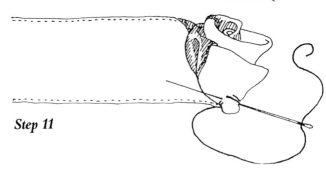

Stitch securely at base and sides as above.

Step 11

These steps are repeated, as shown below, until you achieve desired size of rose.

Step 12

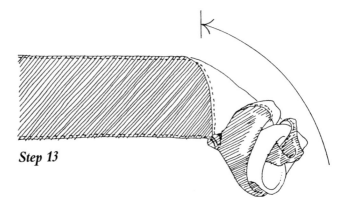

Step 13

Cut ribbon and stitch at base of rose, tucking in corners and raw edges.

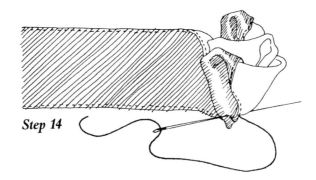

Step 14

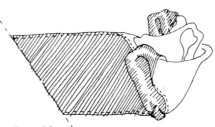

Step 15

Step 16

HOW TO MAKE A TEA ROSE

(As per 'The Rose' Steps 1–14)

Continue to make a tea rose.

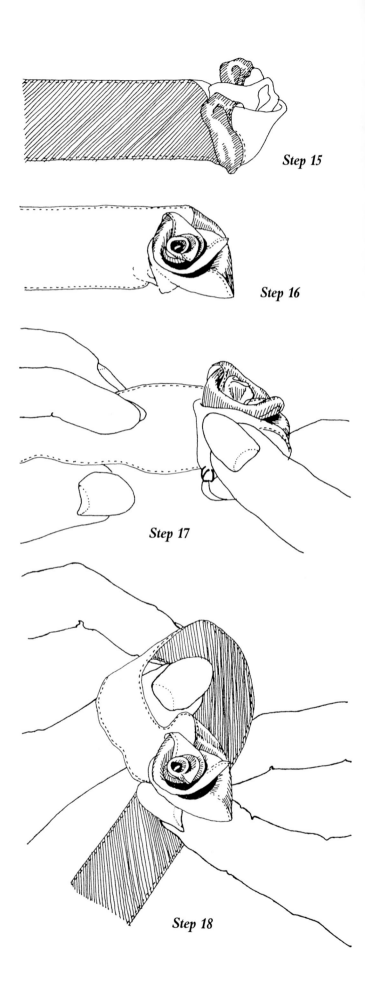

Step 15

Step 16

Do not cut ribbon.

Step 17

Using left hand, loop ribbon length as shown.

Step 18

Stitch to secure at base of rose.

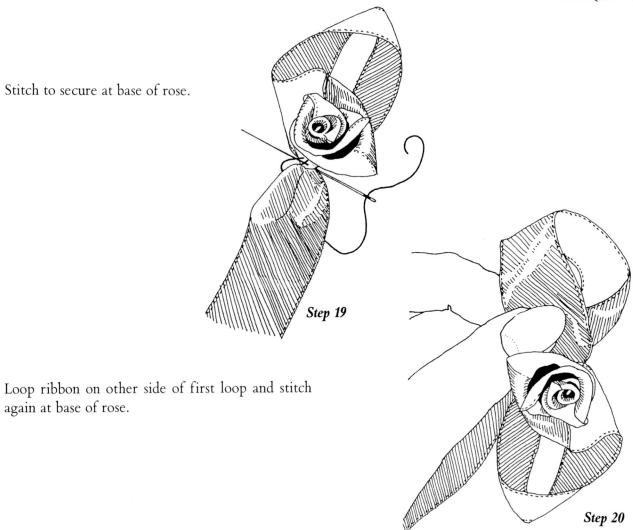

Step 19

Step 20

Loop ribbon on other side of first loop and stitch again at base of rose.

Loop ribbon length as shown and stitch securely.

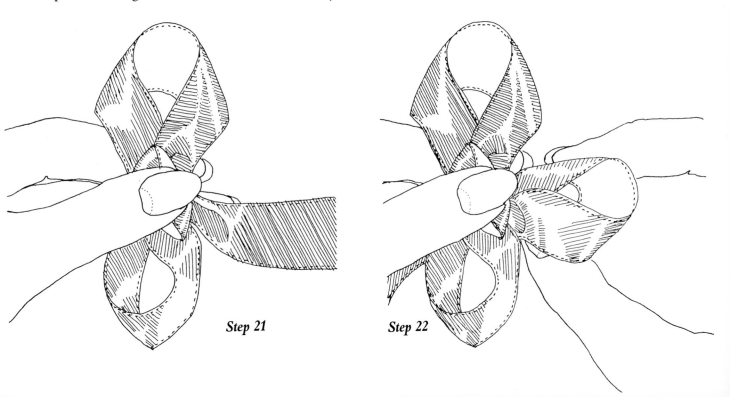

Step 21

Step 22

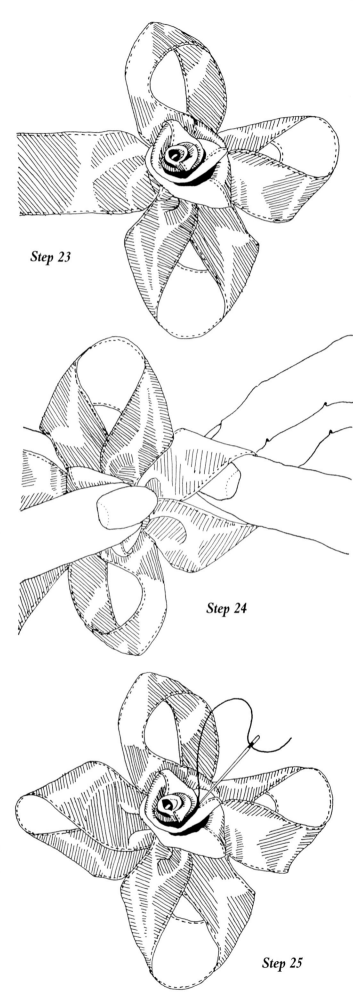

You can make your tea roses larger or more full by repeating these steps in between petals already made.

Step 23

Loop ribbon length as shown to form fourth petal and stitch securely at base. Cut off any excess ribbon.

Fold cut edge over back of rose and stitch securely to hide raw edge.

Step 24

To stitch rose to design, secure centre rose by bringing needle up in the centre rose folds and stitch in place securely, in a few places.

Step 25

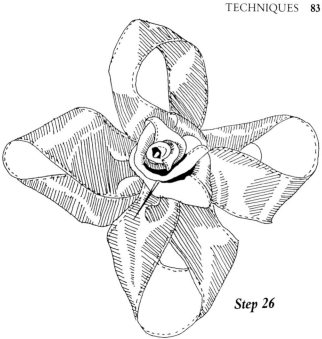

Step 26

The outer petals may be manipulated into the desired shape, using needle and thread to secure them into different positions. The following demonstrates one method but you can experiment with others.

Bring your needle up under the centre point of each outer petal (working on one petal at a time). Using the tip of your needle, pierce the centre lower edge of ribbon and secure.

On the same petal, bring your needle up between the centre of the petal through base fabric at point 'A'. Then pierce centre of the top edge of ribbon and return needle through fabric near 'A'.

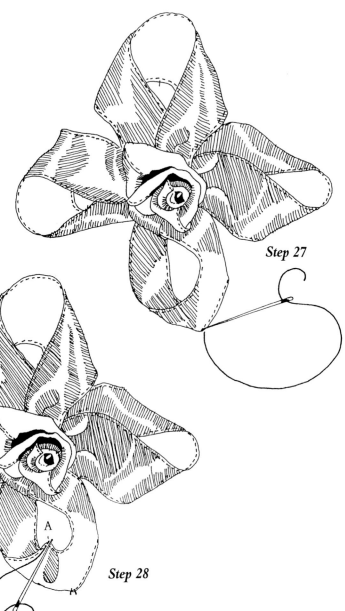

Step 27

Step 28

This method gives a soft rounded petal. Repeat
Step 28 on all petals.

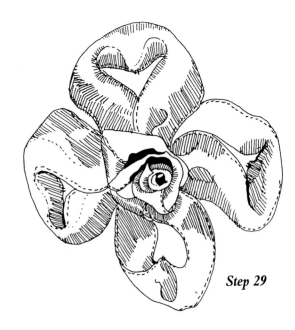

Step 29

RIBBON LILY

(As per 'The Rose' Steps 1–6)

Step 7

Move centre of lily to left of turn in ribbon, to
create a large lily petal.

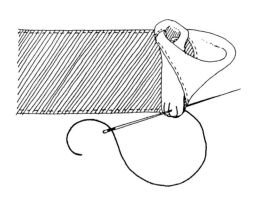

Step 8

Move centre of lily down into the flower — fold
ribbon over away from flower.

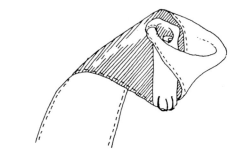

Step 9

Roll ribbon around and away from flower.

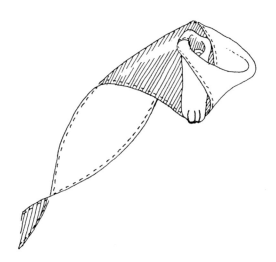

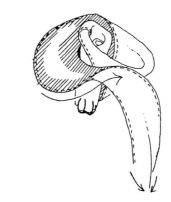

Step 10

Bring curled and folded ribbon around to the base of the flower. Secure at base.

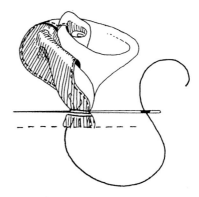

Step 11

Cut excess ribbon, wrap thread around base to secure lily.

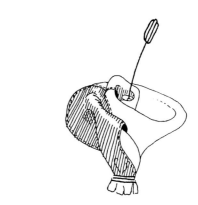

Step 12

Stamens are added after the lilies are secured to the design, by combining one straight stitch and a 'skinny' 'Straight Stitch Bud'.

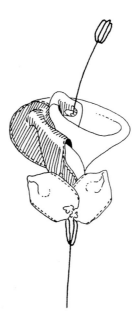

Step 13

Add two 'Straight Stitch' leaves at the base of the lily and a 'Fly Stitch' directly underneath as its stem.

Ribbon Leaves

Step 1

Fold ribbon over into the desired length of the leaf. Cut excess ribbon.

Step 2

Use gathering stitch at raw edge, pull tight.

Step 3

Wrap thread around base of leaf several times at gathering and secure by taking needle through ribbon folds.

Step 4

Stitch base of leaf into desired position on design.

Step 5

Bring needle up at point 'A' and take needle through bottom edge of ribbon loop at point 'B'. Re-enter base cloth at point 'C' and pull tight until loop forms a leaf shape.

Step 6

Stitch leaf in place at tip (point 'D'). (Ensure that unfinished end is hidden under flower.)

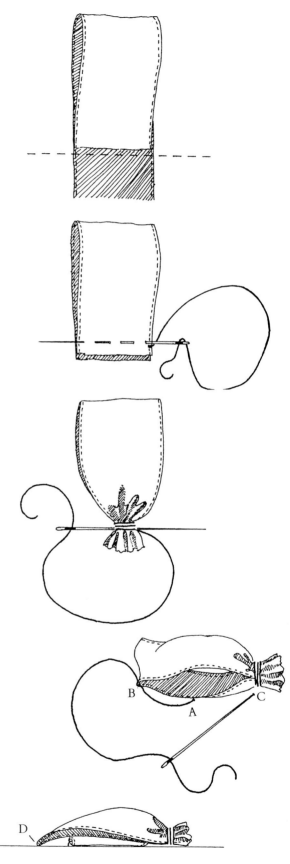

SILK RIBBON BUD

Step 1

Enter design at top point of bud, exit at base of bud to desired height.

Step 2

Guide needle point slightly to the left of the top of the bud, gently draw through, taking care to keep the ribbon straight.

Step 3

Re-enter at base of bud and guide needle point slightly to the right of the top of the bud; gently draw through, taking care to keep the ribbon straight.

Step 4

Re-enter at base of bud — finish bud off on reverse of work (secure with thread).

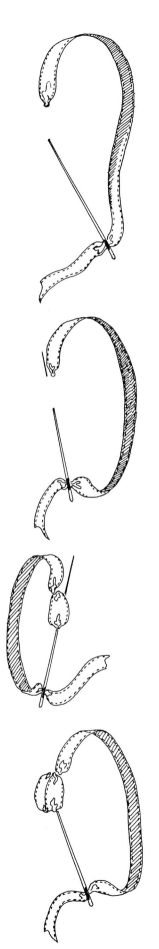

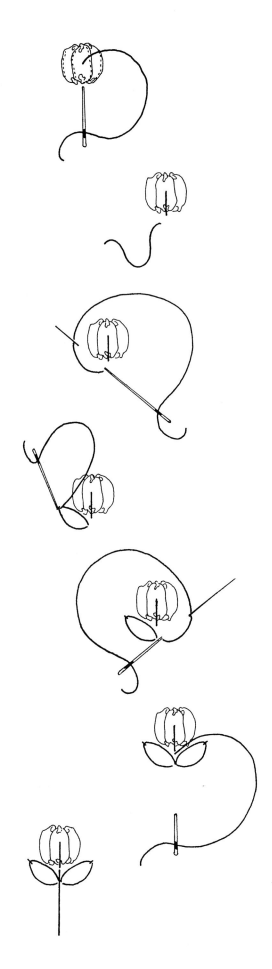

Step 5 To create bud leaves (Lazy Daisy Stitch).

Taking an appropriate thread, pull up through centre of bud and down to the flower's base, draw through gently.

Step 6

Re-enter near the base, but to the left of the bud.

Step 7

Guide needle 'in' beside point where thread comes up (Step 6) and 'out' at the point to the left of the bud which will determine the length of the leaf, ensuring that the loop formed by the thread is caught under the needle.

Step 8

Re-enter cloth on the far side of the loop to secure 'Leaf' in place.

Step 9

Construct second 'Leaf' on right of bud in the same manner as the first leaf.

Step 10

Bring your needle up through the cloth at the base of the bud, re-enter at the point to make the desired stem length.

Step 11

Secure at reverse of design. Finished 'Silk Ribbon Bud'.

STRAIGHT STITCH

Made as per silk ribbon bud up to Step 4.

Step 5

Using a finer material than that of which the Buds are made — from the back of the base cloth enter the design to the left and halfway up the height of the bud. Re-enter at the same point on the right of the bud, this time from the face of the cloth. Bring the point of your needle up at the base of the bud and be sure that your needle passes over the top of the loop created by the thread.

Step 6

Pull through gently. The loop will be caught by the thread and create the 'V' at the base of the bud. Re-enter the cloth at the point which will create the desired length of the bud's stem. Secure at reverse of design.

Step 7

Finished bud.

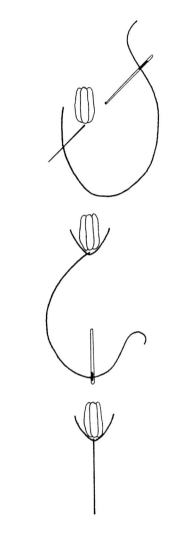

SILK RIBBON ROSETTE STITCH

(Also made with thread)

Step 1

Working anticlockwise in a circular spiral direction (as diagram shows), taking care to keep ribbon flat and stitches very loose.

Step 2

Continue in this fashion around the spiral.

Step 3

Finish rosette with a single loose straight stitch at centre.

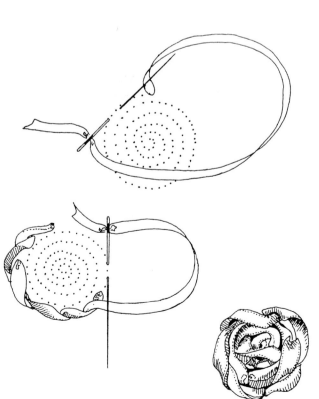

Straight Stitch ribbon Leaf

Step 1

Using a ribbon of the width of the desired leaf, enter the design at either end of the leaf.

Step 2

Re-enter cloth at the other end of the leaf — so creating a leaf of the desired length. Secure ribbon ends at back of work with thread.

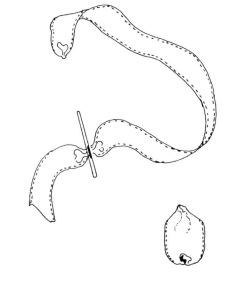

Primrose

Best results achieved with gathered braid.

Step 1

Cut a length of approximately 12 cm.

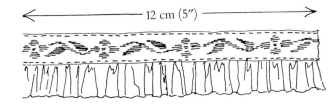

Step 2

Fold braid in half and secure raw edges together.

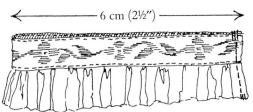

Step 3

Run a gathering stitch along the straight edge of the braid, along the full length of the loop.

Step 4

Draw gathering thread firmly, until a 'Primrose' is formed.

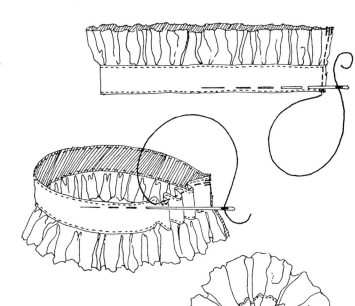

Step 5

Secure the back of the flower with several small stitches.

Reverse Ribbon Leaves

Step 1

Pull needle and ribbon up to the front of the work at the point where the leaf is to be placed.

Step 2

Draw ribbon down, with right side facing, hold in place with your left thumb.

Step 3

Still holding the ribbon in place with your thumb, insert your needle into ribbon and through base cloth.

Step 4

Draw ribbon through carefully, ensuring ribbon does not twist.

Step 5

When ribbon is pulled through, trim and secure at the back of the work.

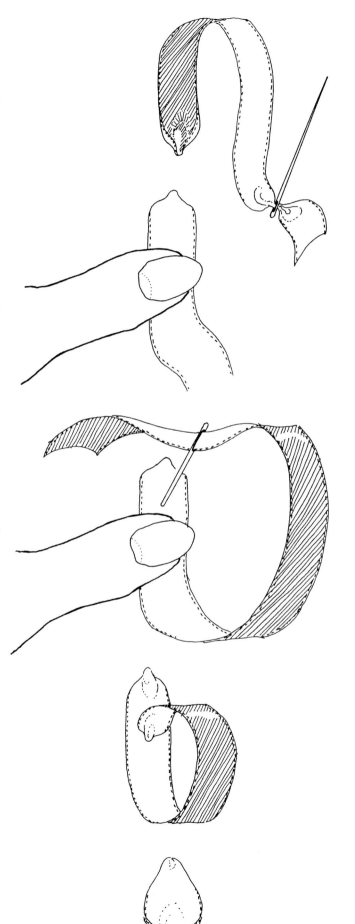

GARDENIAS

Gardenias are made in the same fashion as the tea rose but with more petals; up to eight on any one flower.

LOOPED BOW/LOOPED RIBBON/LOOPED LEAF

Step 1

Bring needle up at point 'A' and re-enter at point 'B', being careful to keep ribbon flat.

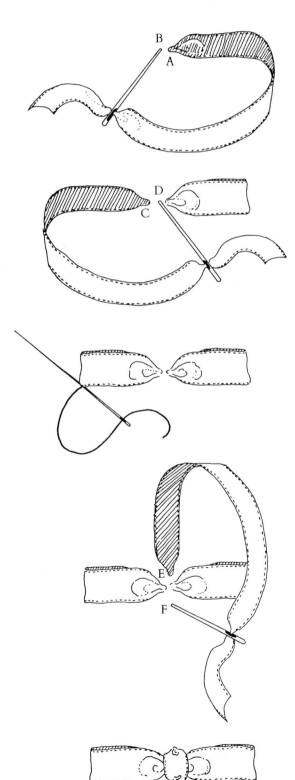

Step 2

Opposite this loop, bring the needle up at point 'C' and re-enter at point 'D', ensuring ribbon is kept flat.

Step 3

Secure tips of 'bow'.

Step 4

For the centre of the bow, bring needle up at point 'E' and re-enter at point 'F', taking care not to allow ribbon to twist.

Step 5

Secure ribbon ends on reverse of work.

Note: For 'Looped Leaf' use Step 1 only and stitch down one corner of ribbon fold.

TWIRLED RIBBON ROSE

Step 1

Bring needle up at point 'A' and draw ribbon through. Hold needle up, keeping the ribbon away from the base cloth.

Step 2

Twirl needle anticlockwise, which in turn will twirl the ribbon.

Step 3

Continue twirling until the ribbon makes a tight coil. (Stop when ribbon starts buckling.)

Step 4

Make a 3 cm (1¼″) loop. Hold taut and close to your work.

Step 5

Let loop go — this will create a double coil. Put needle in at point 'B' and pull through fabric gently until you form desired rose size.

Step 6

These roses need to be secured otherwise they will uncoil, so gently stitch in place — using one strand of cotton with a couple of small stitches.

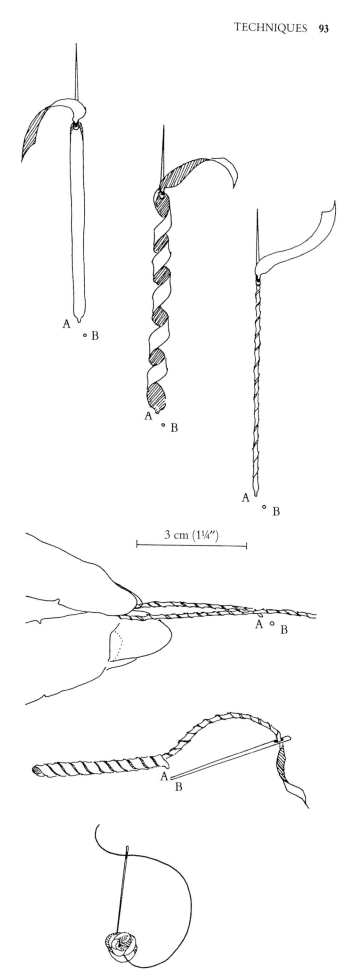

$\mathcal{S}$TITCH GLOSSARY

SHADOW STITCH

This stitch may be used for many shapes, it is not limited to a straight bar. The best effects are achieved using a transparent fabric.

Step 1

(Although you are working to the right, each stitch seen on the 'face' of the design is completed by a backward stitch to the left.)

Choose a point near the end of the image you are working on, bring your needle up at this point 'A'. Still on this edge of the image, make a straight stitch to the left to point 'B'. Guide your needle under the design to the opposite side of the image, ensuring that you come up a little to the right of your first step — point 'C'.

Step 2

Make a straight stitch to point 'D' the left of point 'C'. Guide your needle under the design to the original side of the image to point 'E', ensuring that you come up with a full stitch length to the right of point 'A'.

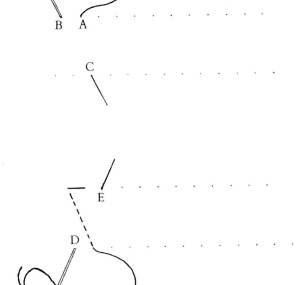

Step 3

Make a straight stitch to point 'F' next to point 'A'. Guide your needle under the design to the opposite side of the image to point 'G'.

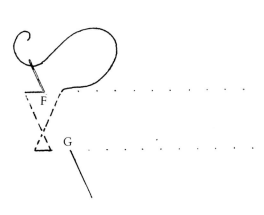

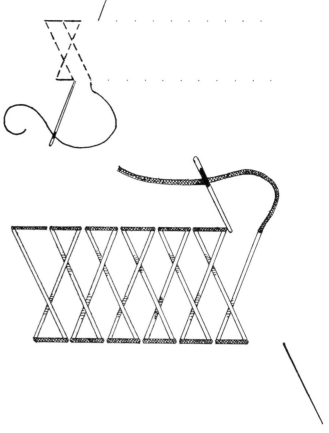

Steps 4 & 5

Continue in this fashion until you have completed the image.

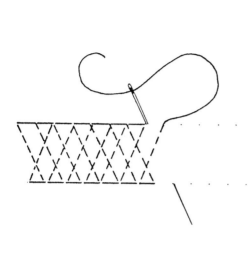

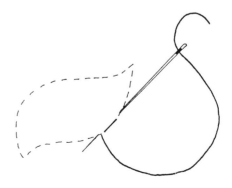

SATIN STITCH

Step 1

Bring the needle and thread to the face of the fabric. Make a backward straight stitch at the edge of the shape to be 'coloured in'.

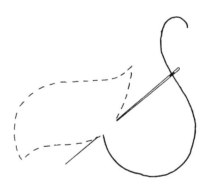

Step 2

Alongside this initial stitch, make another (keeping stitches close to each other).

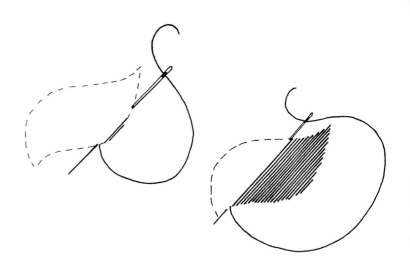

Step 3

Continue working in this fashion.

Step 4

Continue until shape is completed.

FRENCH KNOT

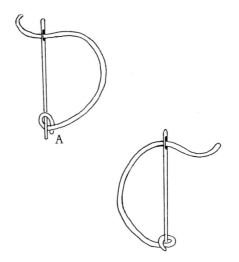

Step 1

Start with thread and needle pulled through to the face of the fabric (point 'A'). Wind the thread around the needle and return the needle into the fabric just beside point 'A'.

Step 2

Gently pull thread through loop and fabric to back of cloth.

Step 3

Secure at back of cloth — finished knot.

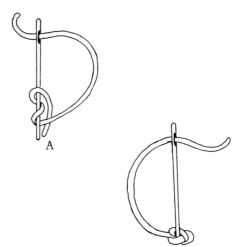

Step 4

For a larger knot, wind the thread around the needle a couple of times. Re-enter at point 'A'.

Step 5

Gently push the needle and thread through to the back of the fabric.

Step 6

Secure at back of fabric. Finished knot.

STEM STITCH

Step 1

Bring your needle and thread up at the beginning of the line or outline. Keep your needle pointing away from the direction you are going. Make one large stitch back and guide the tip of your needle to the point halfway along this stitch.

Step 2

Ensure that the thread is under the point of the needle (see inset diagram). Pull through. Make another backward stitch half the size of the first stitch, bring the tip of the needle up along point 'B' but not into point 'B'.

Step 3

Continue in this manner until you have completed the stem or outline.

LAZY DAISY STITCH

Step 1

Bring the needle and thread up to the face of the cloth. Create a loop, bring the needle back to the original entry point, guiding the tip of the needle to the outer tip of the petal and through. Ensure that the needle passes over the thread (loop).

Step 2

Pull the needle and thread through. Make a tiny straight stitch over the tip of the petal, catching and securing the loop as you go.

Step 3

Repeat steps 1 and 2 around the flower for a simple daisy look.

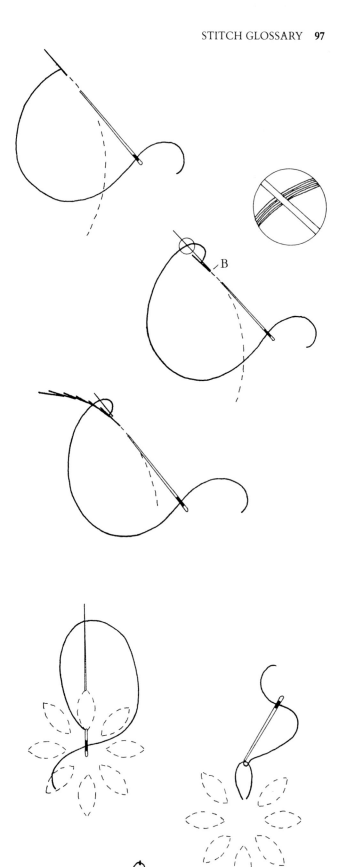

FLY STITCH

Step 1

Bring needle and thread up at point 'A'. Insert needle at point 'B' and guide tip of needle to point 'C'. Ensure that the needle passes over the 'loop' created.

Step 2

Bring the needle and thread over the 'V' shape created, re-enter fabric at point 'D'.

Step 3

Thus creating a 'Y' shape ideal for smaller flowers.

Step 4

Or, alternatively, make a very short 'stem', thus making a 'V' shape.

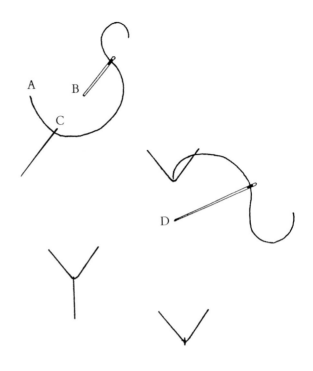

BULLION ROSE STITCH

Step 1

(Usually sewn with the darkest shade of the Rose colour.) Make a backstitch in the centre of points 'A' and 'B' to secure the bullion stitch. Start stitch with thread on right side of fabric, insert needle at the point for the desired stitch length 'B'; guide tip up at point 'A'. Pull needle through until just the eye of the needle is showing; **do not pull thread through.**

Step 2

Wind thread clockwise around needle ensuring the first wrap is close to the base of the needle shaft, do not cross your thread while wrapping — wrap thread loosely.

Step 3

Wind until length of wound thread on the needle will cover the desired length of the stitch (allowing for the thread to 'compact' when pulled through).

Step 4

Place your left thumb over the loose coil on the needle then gently pull the needle and thread through. Keep your thumb on the bullion as it eases forward into position.

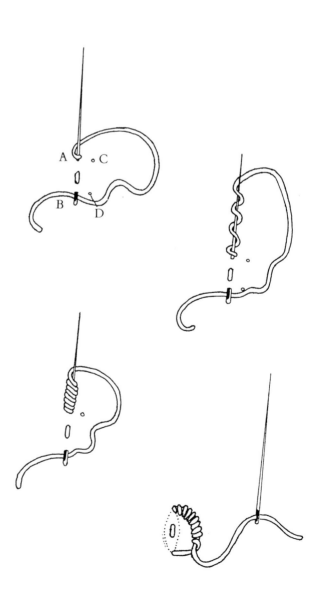

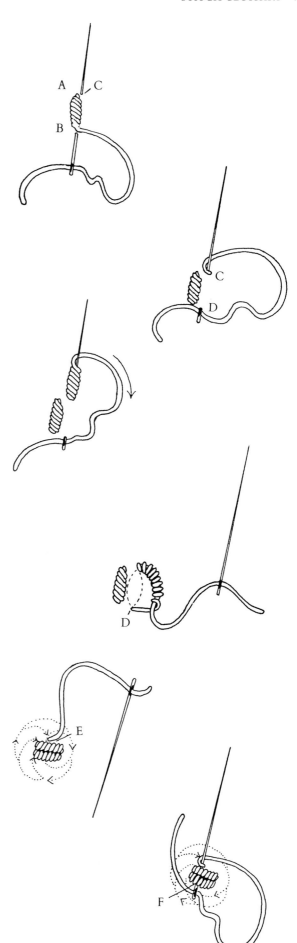

Step 5

To secure the stitch, place your needle just beside (but not in) point 'B', then guide the needle tip up at point 'C' to start your second stitch to the right of the first.

Step 6

Insert needle at the point for the desired stitch length 'D'; guide tip up at point 'C'. Pull needle through until just the eye of the needle is showing; **do not pull thread through.**

Step 7

Wind thread clockwise around needle, ensuring the first wrap is close to the base of the needle shaft. Do not cross your thread while wrapping — wrap thread loosely. Wind until length of wound thread on the needle will cover the desired length of the stitch (allowing for the thread to 'compact' when pulled through).

Step 8

Place your left thumb over the loose coil on the needle, then gently pull the needle and thread through. Keep your thumb on the bullion as it eases forward into position. To secure the stitch, place your needle just beside (but not in) point 'D' secure at the back of the work. The two bullion stitches placed side by side in this fashion create the centre of your rose.

Step 9

(Usually sewn with a medium shade of Rose colour.) Work petals clockwise. To start rose petals bring your needle and thread to the face of the cloth, next to the 'Rose Centre' and half way along its length at point 'E'.

Step 10

Insert needle at the point for the desired stitch length 'F'; guide tip up at point 'E'. Pull needle through until just the eye of the needle is showing; **do not pull thread through.** Wind thread clockwise around needle, ensuring the first wrap is close to the base of the needle shaft.

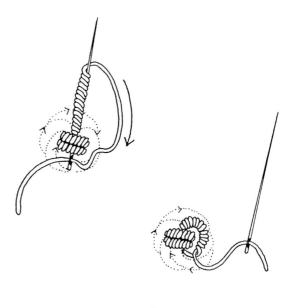

Step 11

Wind thread loosely around needle shaft in a clockwise direction, approximately 16 times.

Step 12

Place your left thumb over the loose coil on the needle then gently pull the needle and thread through. Keep your thumb on the bullion as it eases into position, arching around the centre of the rose.

Step 13

To secure the stitch, place your needle just beside (but not in) point 'F', then guide the needle tip up at point 'E'. To start your second petal bring your needle up at point 'G'.

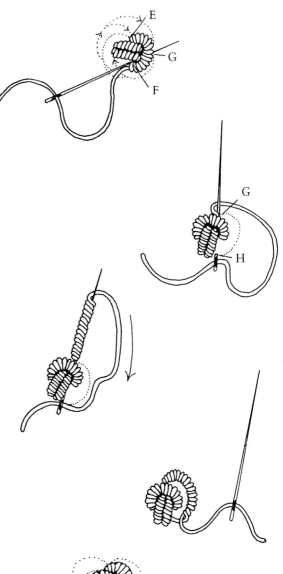

Step 14

Insert needle at the point for the desired stitch length 'H'; guide tip up at point 'G'. Pull needle through until just the eye of the needle is showing; **do not pull thread through.** Wind thread clockwise around needle ensuring the first wrap is close to the base of the needle shaft.

Step 15

Wind thread loosely around needle shaft in a clockwise direction, approximately 16 times.

Step 16

Place your left thumb over the loose coil on the needle then gently pull the needle and thread through. Keep your thumb on the bullion as it eases into position, arching around the centre of the rose.

Step 17

Continue remaining petals in the same fashion.

Step 18

Work until the rose has five petals. Secure at the back of the design.

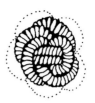

Step 19

(Usually sewn with the palest shade of Rose colour, for a larger rose.) Continue to work petals clockwise. Repeat steps 10 to 18 starting each outer petal halfway along each inner petal, and finishing each outer petal halfway along the next inner petal.

STOCKISTS

VICTORIA

Bartfeld Textiles P/L
576 Glenhuntly Road
Elsternwick 3185
(*Fur fabrics*)

Nancraft
370 Lt Bourke St
Melbourne 3000
(*All states*)

Designer Trim
134 Bridge Road
Richmond 3121
(*Specialist ribbons, trimmings, filigree pieces. All states*)

Bustle & Bows
104 Union Road
Surrey Hills 3127
(*Specialists ribbons, trimmings, fabrics*)

A. Macdougall P/L
9 Cremorne St
Richmond 3121
(*Specialists ribbons, trimmings*)

E. C. Birch P/L
153 Bridge Road
Richmond 3121
(*All haberdashery needs*)

The Button Shop
181 Glenferrie Road
Malvern 3144
(*Excellent range of double-sided satin ribbon and braids*)

Romantique Haberdashery
Kings Arcade
974 High Street
Armadale 3143
(*Specialist ribbons, gold cupids*)

Spotlight
Stores throughout Australia
(*Moire taffeta, silk dupion*)

Franke Stuart P/L
612 Glenferrie Road
Hawthorn 3122
(*Pure silk organza and specialty fabrics*)

Peuan Thai
654 Glenferrie Road
Hawthorn 3122
(*Superb range of Thai silks*)

Horizon Fabrics
186 York Street
South Melbourne 3205
(*Heavy damask and other fabrics*)

Robbyn Macdonald Embroidery
60 North Road
Brighton 3182
(*Chinese silk threads, bread dough brooches, silk pictures*)

Attic Crafts
5A Bath Lane
Bendigo 3550

Port Melbourne Prints & Framing
Bay Street
Port Melbourne 3207
(*Specialist embroidery framers*)

Lincraft
Australia-wide

Painters Window
Kings Arcade
High Street
Armadale 3143

NEW SOUTH WALES

Needlecraft International
96 Rowe Street
Eastwood 2122

Berala Crafts
101 Berala Arcade
Berala 2141

Habycrafts
41 Day Street North
Silverwater 2141

Lyn's Fine Needlework
294 Windsor Road
Baulkham Hills 2153

Bobbins & Lace
Shop 23
Victoria Plaza
369 Victoria Avenue
Chatswood 2067

Lakemba Sewing Wool & Craft Supplies
103 Haldon Street
Lakemba 2195

Simply Stitches
1 Ferguson Lane
Chatswood 2067

Tapestry Craft
32 York Street
Sydney 2000

QUEENSLAND
Art & Craft Supermarket
Capalaba Park Shopping Centre
Capalaba 4157

Bead & Trimming Co.
69 Elizabeth Street
Brisbane 4000

Elizabeth's Spinning Wheel
Shop 5 Village Fair
97 Flockton Street
McDowall 4053

Heirloom Crafts
Shop 53
Garden City Shopping Centre
Upper Mt Gravatt 4122

O'Connors
36a Ainsworth Street
Salsbury 4107

Toowong Craft Centre
Toowong Village Shopping Centre
Sherwood Road
Toowong 4066

Sullivans Haberdashery
3365 Pacific Highway
Springwood 4127

SOUTH AUSTRALIA
Cottage Crafts
462 Fullarton Road
Myrtle Banks 5064

Gaby's Craft Centre
126 Renaissance Arcade
Adelaide 5000

Glenelg Craft Supplies
15 Jetty Road
Glenelg 5043

At-a-Touch Homecrafts
Suite 4 Professional Centre
The Hub
Aberfoyle Park 5159

Needleworld
109 King William Road
Hyde Park 5061

Daphne's Craft Shoppe
Shop 3 663 Grange Road
Grange 5022

J. Coombe & K. Thompson
14 Avenue Road
Highgate 5063
(*Bread dough brooches & embroidery pieces*)

TASMANIA
U-Do-Haberdashery & Craft
Shop 16A
Northgate Shopping Centre
Glenorchy 7010

The Needlewoman
Shop 23
22 Channel Court
Kingston 7050

Little Stitches
Shop 37 Mayfair in the Bay
236 Sandy Bay Road
Sandy Bay 7005

WESTERN AUSTRALIA
The Silver Thimble
27 Bruce Street
Nedlands 6009

Calico House
2 Napoleon Street
Cottesloe 6010

Knightcraft
25 Yampi Way
Willeton 6155

Arts & Crafts Corner
34 Mint Street
East Victoria Park 4567